Financial Management
in the Public Sector

Financial Management in the Public Sector

Tools, Applications, and Cases

XiaoHu Wang

M.E.Sharpe
Armonk, New York
London, England

Copyright © 2006 by M.E. Sharpe, Inc.

Screen shots reprinted by
permission from Microsoft Corporation.

Library of Congress Cataloging-in-Publication Data

Wang, XiaoHu, 1962-
  Financial management in the public sector : tools, applications, and cases
/ by XiaoHu Wang.
      p. cm.
  Includes bibliographical references and index.
  ISBN 0-7656-1677-7 (cloth : alk. paper) — ISBN 0-7656-1678-5 (pbk.: alk. paper)
  1. Finance, Public. 2. Finance, Public—Accounting. 3. Budget. I. Title.

HJ141.W36 2006
352.4—dc22   2005024995

Printed in the United States of America

The paper used in this publication meets the minimum requirements of
American National Standard for Information Sciences
Permanence of Paper for Printed Library Materials,
ANSI Z 39.48-1984.

∞

BM (c) 10   9   8   7   6   5   4   3   2   1
BM (p) 10   9   8   7   6   5

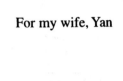

For my wife, Yan

Contents

List of Illustrations

Tables

Figures

Excel Screens

Preface and Acknowledgments

I always ask a few questions before buying a book. What is the book about? Why did the author write it? How are important topics covered? I use this preface to answer some questions that may be in the mind of a possible reader.

Why Did I Write this Book?

I wrote this book because I want the reader to use it, not just read it. This is a book about application. It is about using what is learned. During my decade-long teaching experience on financial management and budgeting, I have learned that two things really stimulate student learning. One is an instructor's interest in student learning. Another, more important factor, is application of the materials. If students know they will *use* what they learn, they are more interested in learning it. This book emphasizes the application of budgeting and financial management tools in the real world. Its goal is to familiarize students with the application of analytical tools to resolve financial management and budgeting issues.

How Are Applications Emphasized in this Book?

The book uses a case study approach to illustrate the application of financial management and budgeting concepts and tools. Each chapter starts with a discussion of a tool (or tools) and related concepts, with examples. It then presents a factual case study to demonstrate the use of the tool(s). The chapter ends with a list of exercise questions. This presentation method is the result of my longtime experience teaching analytical techniques, which often require repetitive examples, cases, and exercises for student learning and application. This method stresses the importance of the case study. The case study allows students to understand the conditions under which a tool can be properly used. It also stimulates student interest and learning by relating the tools to a real-world scenario. Each case study here presents a step-by-step guide to application. A case starts with a presentation of a decision-making scenario in which a tool can be applied, and then demonstrates its application in solving the problem, step by step. The exercises reinforce student understanding of the tools. Exercises also allow students to experience possible variations of a tool.

Microsoft® Excel™ spreadsheet software is used as an example in assisting students in financial calculation. Financial calculation is a critical part of budgeting and financial management, but is often ignored by textbooks. Since the processes of many calculations are complex, the use of computer software or financial calculators is necessary. Excel is a popular and powerful software program for financial calculation. This book provides step-by-step examples of Excel programming for many tools. The use of Excel can save students time in calculating and enables the instructor to teach calculation-sophisticated tools that they couldn't teach otherwise.

What Is Covered in this Book?

The material is covered in three sections: financial planning, financial implementation, and financial reporting and analysis. In the financial planning section, the focus is on how to project and develop financial resources (Chapter 1: Revenue Forecasting; Chapter 2: Resource Development Analysis), and on how to plan and improve resource use (Chapter 3: Cost Estimation; Chapter 4: Cost Comparison; Chapter 5: Incremental Cost Analysis; Chapter 6: Cost-Benefit Analysis).

The focus in the financial implementation section is on tools to detect and correct undesirable financial operations, and on tools to ensure continuation of normal financial activities (Chapter 7: Financial Performance Monitoring). Tools to monitor cash flows are also covered in this section (Chapter 8: Cash Management: Determining the Optimal Cash Balance).

In the financial reporting and analysis section, the material stresses how to use financial information to analyze and improve the financial condition of an organization. This section highlights the two most important financial reports in state and local governments: The Statement of Net Assets (Chapter 9) and The Statement of Activities (Chapter 10). It also presents financial reporting at the fund level (Chapter 11). The last chapter discusses the tool to evaluate the financial condition of a government (Chapter 12).

What Were the Criteria for Selecting Topics to Cover?

First, a topic must be important in public financial management and budgeting. Financial managers are frequently asked to forecast revenues, evaluate revenue potentials, compare and evaluate costs, monitor financial performance, manage cash flows, and conduct financial analysis. These topics are included in the book. Second, a topic must be analytical in nature, which means that a technical solution is needed and financial calculation is involved. Therefore, simple subjects such as drafting a budget request, determining budget line-item classifications, or preparing a spreadsheet of revenue (or expense) summary are not included.

Although the book does not provide comprehensive coverage of all tools in public budgeting and finance, the analytical processes covered in the book should be generic enough that the reader can relate and develop a good knowledge on analytical tools used in public budgeting and financial management.

Who Should Use the Book?

The book can be used as a supplementary textbook in a public budgeting or a public financial management course. It can supplement a textbook that mainly covers theories. It can also be used as a main textbook for a public financial management course that focuses on application of budgeting and financial management tools. Teachers of analytical techniques courses can also consider it as recommended reading. Finally, it can be used by financial and budget personnel in governments, or anyone who is interested in governmental finance.

What Is the Math Requirement for the Reader?

As the calculations can be performed using Excel, the math requirement for the reader is minimal. A reader can readily understand the materials and exercises with a basic knowledge of high school algebra.

Acknowledgments

I am very grateful to many people for their support, encouragement, and suggestions. First, I want to thank the people I worked with at M.E. Sharpe for their support: Harry Briggs, Elizabeth Granda, and Jennifer Morettini. I thank my previous and current colleagues at the University of Central Florida for their support and encouragement. I especially thank Lynda M. Dennis, who read through a draft of this book and provided many valuable suggestions. I also thank the students in my financial management courses for their feedback, and Jeff Tu for providing research assistance. Finally, special thanks are reserved for my wife, Yan, whose love and support are an everlasting source of inspiration for me.

PART I

TOOLS FOR FINANCIAL PLANNING

CHAPTER 1

Revenue Forecasting

Learning Objectives

After studying this chapter, you should be able to

- Use forecasting tools presented in this chapter
- Determine forecast accuracy
- Apply the most accurate tool for forecasting

Why forecast revenue? Revenue forecasting helps financial planning. Because revenue determines service capacity, accurate revenue forecasting allows for a good understanding of an organization's ability to provide services. Forecasting is also a process through which managers learn about their communities and organizations. For example, how much of a community's resources can be used to provide services in demand? How capable is the organization of collecting these resources? A poor forecast—a large gap between the forecast and actual revenues—warrants a close look at a community's resource potentials and an organization's revenue collection efforts.

Who does forecasting? It is often the responsibility of budget offices or central management offices. Sometimes, individual agencies that have their own resources, such as businesslike enterprise functions in many governments, also forecast their revenues.

What forecasting tools are available? A variety of qualitative and quantitative tools are used in revenue forecasting. The Delphi technique is perhaps the most popular qualitative tool. It is a process in which a group of experts are individually questioned about their perceptions of future events that will affect the revenue flows. Each expert gives a forecasting figure and presents a rationale, and then an outside party summarizes these forecasts and rationales and comes back to the experts with more questions. The process continues until a collective forecast is reached.

Quantitative forecast tools vary from simple smoothing techniques to sophisticated causal modeling. It should be noted that mathematical

Table 1.1

Forecasting Example One

Year	1	2	3	4	5	6	7	8
Revenues ($)	12.00	14.00	17.00	13.00	17.00	14.00	16.00	?

sophistication is not a guarantee of forecast accuracy. In this chapter we introduce quantitative tools that are simple to understand and easy and inexpensive to use. They are also the proper techniques for most revenue sources in governments.

Concepts and the Tool

Before forecasting, several things need to be determined. First, the *forecast subject*—what is being forecast—must be decided. Is a tax, a fee, or a user charge being forecasted? Is the forecast for the whole organization/jurisdiction, or just a part of it? Second, a *forecast horizon*—the length of the forecast—must be established. Should revenue be projected for the next month, the next year, or the next five years?

Third, the forecaster must become familiar with *forecasting techniques* in order to select one that is proper for the forecasting need. This selection involves a comparison of the forecast accuracies of different techniques in order to choose the most accurate one. In this chapter, we study several forecasting techniques that have proven effective, simple to understand, and inexpensive to apply. They are simple moving average (SMA), exponential smoothing (EXS), transformation moving average (TMA), regression against time, and a quasi-causal technique. We can use Microsoft® Excel™ spreadsheet software to help us in these calculations. Excel is a spreadsheet program that can be used to perform quantitative and financial calculations. It is very popular and easy to use. If you are not comfortable with it, take a look at an introductory guide to the software. You should be ready in no time. First, let us look at an example. The historical revenue information for a hypothetical organization over the last seven years is shown in Table 1.1. Using this information, forecast the revenue of the eighth year.

Simple Moving Average (SMA)

Using the simple moving average (SMA) technique, we calculate the arithmetic average of revenues in previous *forecast periods* ("years" in this case) and use it as the forecast. To do so, we need first to determine the number of forecast periods in calculation. Let us say that we want an average of the previous five years, then the forecast for the eighth year is (17.00 + 13.00 + 17.00 + 14.00 + 16.00)/5 = 15.40. Similarly, a six-year average is (14.00 + 17.00 + 13.00 + 17.00 + 14.00 + 16.00)/6 = 15.17.

SMA is very simple to understand and easy to use. But it has a major drawback—it weighs all previous revenues equally in averaging. In other words, it treats the revenue from ten years ago as if it is as important as last year's revenue. Common sense says that we should place more weight on the more recent revenue. It is like predicting the outcome of a ballgame. A team's more recent performance should carry more weight in prediction. A team that won *recently* is the favorite to win again. But that is not the case for SMA. SMA assigns the same weight to all data in averaging. In the above example, each figure in the five-year average is assigned a weight factor of one-fifth. We will come back to this point later in this chapter.

We can use Excel to calculate SMA. The following is the Excel programming to calculate SMA.

Step 1: Open up a new Excel file. Notice that a sheet is designed for data input in columns and rows. Columns are named by letter; rows are named by number. A particular cell can be located by using a letter and a number such as A1, B2, and so forth. Now, input the revenue data in Column A as shown in Excel Screen 1.1.

Step 2: Click "Data Analysis" under the "Tools" function. (Note: You may need to "Add-In" the data analysis function in "Tools." To do that, go to "Tools" function, select "add-in" and click "Analysis ToolPak.")

Step 3: Select "Moving Average" in the "Data Analysis" window.

Step 4: Select Column A as your "Input Range."

Step 5: Enter 5 in "Interval," as we used five periods in the above example.

Step 6: Select Column B as your "Output Range."

Step 7: Click "OK." You should see the forecast SMA figures in Column B.

Excel will provide you with three forecasting figures based on the selection of five different periods. The average of the first five figures is 14.60. The average of the second five figures is 15.00. The forecast of the most recent five figures is 15.40.

Exponential Smoothing (EXS)

The exponential smoothing (EXS) technique assigns different weights to data of different periods. It allows us to assign larger weights to the more recent

Excel Screen 1.1   **Simple Moving Average**

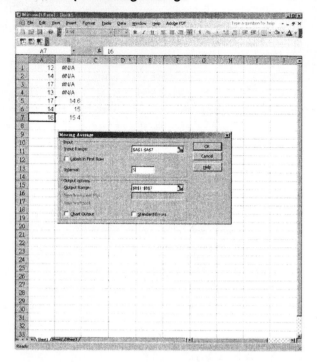

data. In the above example, we can give a large weight, say 40 percent (or 0.40), to the most recent revenue, 16.00; we can assign the other 60 percent to the average of the previous six years, which is (12.00 + 14.00 + 17.00 + 13.00 + 17.00 + 14.00)/6 = 14.50. Therefore, the forecast is (0.40)(16.00) + (0.60)(14.50) = 15.10.

Realize that the sum of the weights needs to be 1.0 (0.4 + 0.6), or 100 percent. In this example, we use a six-period average. You can choose a three-period average with the same assignment of weights. The average is (13.00 + 17.00 + 14.00)/3 = 14.67. So, the forecast is (0.40)(16.00) + (0.60)(14.67) = 15.20. Forecasters call the weight 0.40 a *smoothing constant,* or α (alpha is Greek letter a), and they use the following equation in forecasting:

$$F_{t+1} = \alpha\, A_t + (1 - \alpha)\, F_t$$

In the equation, t is the current period and $t +1$ is the next period. F_{t+1} is the forecast for the next period. A_t is the actual revenue of the current period. F_t is the average (or smoothed) revenue of previous periods. The Excel data analysis package has a function for EXS. The programming is similar to that of SMA.

Excel Screen 1.2 **Exponential Smoothing**

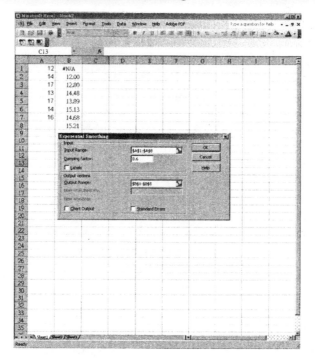

Step 1: Input the revenue data in a column of an Excel spreadsheet as shown in Excel Screen 1.2.

Step 2: Click "Data Analysis" under the "Tools" function.

Step 3: Select "Exponential Smoothing" in the "Data Analysis" window.

Step 4: In the "Exponential Smoothing" window, make sure you highlight eight cells (one more than the original seven years of revenue) in your data column as your "Input Range." This is important, as you are forecasting the revenue of Year 8.

Step 5: The "Damping Factor" in Excel is $1 - \alpha$. In the above example, we type in 0.60 (1 – 0.40).

Step 6: Select eight cells of the column adjacent to your data as the "Output Range."

Step 7: Click "OK."

Excel provides a series of smoothed revenue forecasts: 12.00, 12.80, 14.48, 13.89, 15.13, 14.68, and 15.21. Notice that Excel defines F_t as "smoothed" revenue, not "average" as in our previous calculation, so the forecasts are a little different. In fact, the Excel forecast for Year 8 is $(0.40)(16.00) + (0.60)(14.68) =$

Table 1.2

Forecasting Example Two

Year	1	2	3	4	5	6
Revenues ($)	10.00	13.00	14.00	17.00	19.00	?

15.21. This forecast is a little different from our previous forecast of 15.20, but both are correct. We just need to be aware of different F_t values used.

How to determine α? The values of α go from 0 to 1. The value of 1 indicates that the most recent revenue is used as the forecast; the value of 0 suggests that the most recent revenue is not considered in forecasting. We also know that a larger α indicates a larger weight assigned to the most recent revenue data. However, there is no rule on what α is best. A good method of selecting α is by trial and error, in which you try different αs (from 0 to 1) for a revenue and select the α that gives the most accurate forecast. Later in this chapter, we will learn about a tool to determine the most accurate forecast method. The tool can be used to determine the α.

Like SMA, EXS is also simple to understand. However, it has a major drawback. Let us look at the example in Table 1.2.

What is the forecast for Year 6? A cursory review tells us it has a very good chance of being larger than 19.00. Why? Because the data show an *upward trend*—the revenues have been increasing each year. So history has been repeated again and again, and there is no reason to believe that it won't repeat this time. Now, let us use EXS with $\alpha = 0.80$ (a very large weight on the latest figure 19.00) and a three-period average. The forecast is $(0.80)(19.00) + (0.20)[(13.00 + 14.00 + 17.00)/3] = 18.13$.

We have a forecast figure smaller than 19.00. Very likely, we have *underforecast*—the forecast is smaller than the actual. This happens because EXS *averages* past data in their smoothing. For the same token, if we have a *downward trend*—the revenues have been getting smaller over time—EXS will *overforecast*. The forecast is larger than the actual (if you don't believe me, try EXS on downward data). An important point is that, when revenues show trends of increase or decrease over time, EXS may not provide the most accurate forecast. We will have to look at other techniques for accurate forecasts of revenue trends.

Transformation Moving Average (TMA)

A *trend* occurs when the revenue shows a distinctive direction over time. A positive trend is upward: the revenue gets larger over time. On the other hand, a negative trend shows a downward direction over time.

Table 1.3

Incremental Changes in TMA

Year to year	Increment ($)
1 to 2	13.00 – 10.00 = 3.00
2 to 3	14.00 – 13.00 = 1.00
3 to 4	17.00 – 14.00 = 3.00
4 to 5	19.00 – 17.00 = 2.00

In TMA, we take the trend into consideration by computing *incremental changes* over time. Let us use the data in Table 1.2 to illustrate this technique. The incremental changes are shown in Table 1.3.

We then need to average the increments to get an average increment. In this case, it is (3.00 + 1.00 + 3.00 + 2.00)/4 = 2.25. The forecast revenue in Year 6 is the most recent actual, 19.00 in Year 5, plus this increment, which is 19.00 + 2.25 = 21.25. TMA is a very simple technique. In general, it is more accurate than SMA and EXS for trend data.

Regression Against Time (Regression)

Like TMA, regression is a trend technique. In regression, a relationship is established between revenue and forecast periods (years, months, and so forth) in the following fashion:

$$\text{Forecast revenue} = a + b \text{ (forecast period)}$$

In the equation, a is baseline revenue. It means the revenue without any forecast period (i.e., the forecast period is equal to 0). b is the revenue increment in response to the change in forecast period. It indicates the revenue change from one period to another. Also, in regression language, forecast revenue is designated by Y and the forecast period is designated by X. Hand calculation of a and b is difficult, so we will use Excel. Let us use the data in Table 1.2.

Step 1: Input "Year" in Column A and "Revenue" in Column B in an Excel data sheet as shown in Excel Screen 1.3.
Step 2: Go to "Tools" and select "Data Analysis."
Step 3: Select "Regression" in the "Data Analysis" window.
Step 4: In the "Regression" window, select the "Revenue" column to be Y and the "Year" column to be X. Then select an output range below the original data.
Step 5: Click "OK." The Excel output is shown in Screen 1.3.

Excel Screen 1.3 **Regression Against Time**

The Excel output presents three boxes of results—regression statistics, ANOVA (analysis of variance), and coefficients and their related statistics. All we need is the last box, which gives coefficients of intercept and X variable. The coefficient of intercept is $a;$ the coefficient of X variable is b. In our example, a is 8.00 and b is 2.20, so the regression model is that forecast revenue = 8.00 + 2.20 (Year).

The equation basically means that the revenue has a baseline of 8.00 and an annual increase of 2.20. So the forecast is 8.00 + 2.20(1) = 10.2 for the first year, 8.00 + 2.20(2) = 12.4 for the second year, 8.00 + 2.20(3) = 14.6 for the third year, and so forth. Therefore, the forecast for the sixth year is 8.00 + 2.20 (6) = 21.20.

Regression forecasting may be more accurate for trend data than SMA and EXS, but it is more expensive to use. It often requires computer support. It can be technically and conceptually challenging for forecasters. Also, no evidence shows that it is more accurate than TMA for trend data.

A Quasi-Causal Forecasting Model

So far we have studied SMA, EXS, TMA, and regression techniques. All of these techniques use historical revenue information in forecasting. For instance, in the example in Table 1.2, we used historical data of the past five years to predict the revenue of Year 6. The techniques that use historical data of revenue in forecasting are called *time-series* forecasting techniques, and the historical data are called time-series data.

In some cases, however, time-series revenue data simply do not exist, or the data exist but have limitations that significantly affect their utility. For example, data may be missing for certain years in the past. Two revenue sources may be merged in the past to create a new revenue category. Tax rate or tax base may have changed significantly in the past to reflect a new revenue need. Under these circumstances, the use of time-series data in forecasting is either impossible or improper. We need to consider other tools.

If we can identify several *predictors* that are highly associated with revenue, we can use these predictors in forecasting. For example, if we know the tax base and tax rate of a specific tax, then the tax revenue is the product of tax base and tax rate. Tax base and tax rate are predictors of tax revenue. If we use T for tax revenue, B for tax base, and R for tax rate, then

$$T = B \times R$$

In a local property tax example, suppose that total assessed taxable property value (i.e., tax base) in a city is $10,000,000 this year, and that the city's property tax rate is $5 for every $ 1,000 assessed taxable value (i.e., the millage = 5). The forecast property tax revenue for this year is $10,000,000 \times 5/1,000 = \$50,000$.

This tool may be accurate for short-period forecasting (one to three years). It probably is more accurate for revenues whose predicators can be controlled to some degree. For example, in the above example, if local property tax rates are determined by a local government, forecasters in that government will know the rates for the forecast period, and the forecast could be more accurate because of reduced uncertainty in forecasting.

Determining Forecast Accuracy

How accurate is our forecast? To answer this question, we can use two measures: the absolute percentage error (APE) and the mean absolute percentage error (MAPE). These measures estimate the difference of the forecast from the actual revenue. A smaller actual-versus-forecast difference indicates more accurate forecasting.

$$APE = \frac{|F - A|}{A}$$

Table 1.4

Franchise Taxes in City of Sunburn (in thousands)

Year	1	2	3	4	5	6	7
Revenues ($)	14,305	15,088	15,256	16,748	17,554	18,625	?

Table 1.5

Incremental Changes of Franchise Taxes in City of Sunburn
(in thousands)

Year	1	2	3	4	5
Revenue ($)	14,305	15,088	15,256	16,748	17,554
Increments ($)		783	168	1,492	806

F is the forecast revenue; A is the actual revenue. $//$ is the absolute sign, and any number coming out of it is positive. APE is the forecast-actual difference in percentage. A smaller APE indicates a more accurate forecast. APE is simple to understand and easy to use, but it does not tell the direction of forecast error: whether it is an underestimate or overestimate. Let us look at an example. The actual revenue receipts for franchise taxes in the city of Sunburn are shown in Table 1.4.

Let us say that we want to forecast the revenue at Year 7 (next year). But before forecasting, we want to know the accuracy of different forecasting techniques so we can use the most accurate one. We first scan the data and find an upward trend. So we limit our selection to trend forecasting techniques: TMA or regression. Now, if our goal is to choose a more accurate technique, which is better—TMA or regression?

First, let us compute APE for TMA. We know that, to get APE, we need both the actual revenue and the forecast revenue. We know the actual revenue at Year 6 was $18,625, and we also know the increments before that year, shown in Table 1.5.

The TMA forecast of Year 6 revenue, with the two most recent increments, is $17,554 + ($806 + $1,492)/2 = $18,703. So APE for TMA is: $APE_{TMA} =$ | $18,703 – $18,625 | /$18,625 = 0.0042, or 0.42 percent.

Now, let us get the APE for the regression forecast. The regression equation with the revenues for the first five years is (use Excel for calculation): Revenue = $13,343 + $816 (Year). So the forecast at Year 6 is $13,343 + $816(6) = $18,239, and then $APE_{Regression}$ = | $18,239 – $18,625 |/$18,625 = 0.0207, or 2.07 percent.

APE_{TMA} is smaller than $APE_{Regression}$. We can say that TMA is more accurate for this revenue. But, should we choose TMA to forecast? Not quite yet.

To increase the reliability of our results, we need to get MAPE. MAPE is the average (or mean) of multiple APEs.

First, let us look at the MAPE for TMA. In the above example, we used the revenues from the first–five years to forecast the revenue at Year 6 and then to compute the APE. We can call that figure APE_{TMA1}. Similarly, we can also use the revenues from the first–four years to forecast the revenue at Year 5, which was $16,748 + ($1,492 + $168)/2 = $17,578, and then compute another APE—let us call it APE_{TMA2}. APE_{TMA2} = | $17,578 – $17,554 |/ $17,554 = 0.0014, or 0.14 percent. Therefore, $MAPE_{(TMA1 + TMA2)}$ = (0.0042 + 0.0014)/2 = 0.0028, or 0.28 percent.

We can use the same reasoning to compute $MAPE_{(TMA1 + TMA2 + TMA3)}$ and more MAPEs, depending on data availability. Similarly, we can calculate MAPE for regression. Using the first four revenue data to forecast the revenue at Year 5, we have the following regression forecast: revenue = $13,475 + $750(year). So, the forecast is $13,475 + $750(5) = $17,225. $APE_{Regression 2}$ = | $17,225 – $17,554 |/$17,554 = 0.0187, or 1.87 percent. Since $APE_{Regression 1}$ is 0.0207 (see the APE calculation above), the MAPE for regression is $MAPE_{(Regression 1 + Regression 2)}$ = (0.0207 + 0.0187)/2 = 0.0197, or 1.97 percent.

Because $MAPE_{(TMA1 + TMA2)}$ is smaller than $MAPE_{(Regression 1 + Regression 2)}$, we can say that TMA is a more accurate tool and should be used in forecasting the franchise tax in the city.

A Case Study

Sunnytown (population 50,259), Florida, has experienced rapid growth over the past decade. The general fund revenue has grown for the last decade from $6.7 million to $24.7 million. However, annual revenue growth has slowed recently from 20 percent a decade ago to an average of under 5 percent for the past several years. During this time, the intergovernmental revenue from the state and the federal government has grown but become increasingly unstable. Moreover, the town's fiscally conservative leadership has been unwilling to raise property taxation significantly.

The service demand increase and revenue growth decrease have given impetus to the need for enhanced forecast accuracy, particularly in the utility taxes, which have ranged between 15 percent and 18.5 percent of general revenue over the past ten years.

Local officials have found utility taxes difficult to predict in absolute and relative terms, particularly when compared with local property taxation. To forecast utility taxes, the finance director has relied on his own judgment, using data from the past five years, in consultation with other financial officials. The MAPE for utility taxes for the ten-year period was 9.1 percent. To

Table 1.6

Utility Taxes in Sunnytown, Florida

Year	Revenues ($)
1	842,387
2	1,665,430
3	1,863,296
4	2,063,103
5	2,905,717
6	2,994,785
7	3,281,836
8	3,766,661
9	3,907,110
10	4,063,555
11	?

the finance director, forecast errors within plus or minus 5 percent are acceptable. This makes the city's forecast performance in utility taxes significantly below par by its own benchmark. The annual actual utility tax receipts for the past ten years are shown in Table 1.6. What are the forecast utility taxes for the next year (Year 11)?

Step 1: Cleaning the Data

Certain events can significantly impact revenues. A new assessment of taxable properties changes the property tax base and property tax revenues. A water rate change does the same to water fee receipts. The annexation of a neighborhood can also increase a city's revenue base. These events may change revenues at certain times significantly, creating a so-called data *outlier*—obvious deviation from the mainstream revenue trend. In forecasting, these outliers often lead to inaccurate forecasts; therefore they need to be "cleaned" before forecasting.

Quite often, through reviewing the data we can easily spot an outlier (otherwise, why call it an outlier?). A drastic change (increase or decrease) in revenue deserves an investigation. If a change is temporary, such as adoption of a special rate in a particular year, then the revenue needs to be justified on a regular rate basis. If a change is permanent or long-term, then we should consider exclusion of data prior to the change in forecasting.

Our utility data shows a dramatic increase from $842,387 in Year 1 to $1,665,430 in Year 2 (a 97.7 percent increase!). A review of the record shows a utility rate increase during that year from 6 percent to 10 percent. The utility tax has remained 10 percent since then. To clean the impact of the outlier, we can either exclude $842,387 from our forecast, or justify the revenue on a 10 percent rate basis by multiplying a *modifier.* In this case, the modifier justifies the revenue on a 6 percent rate basis to a 10 percent in the following way: modified revenue = actual revenue × modifier. Using our data, this comes to $842,387 × (10 percent/6 percent) = $1,403,978.

Step 2: Choosing the Forecasting Technique

Two factors should be considered in selecting forecast tools: forecast accuracy and cost. The former is more important. First, an acceptable accuracy range should be established (e.g., a MAPE of 5 percent). Notice that it is more difficult to accurately forecast some revenues than others. In general, economy-sensitive revenues, such as sales taxes, fees, and user charges, are more difficult to forecast than property taxes. There should be a consideration to adopt different acceptable accuracy ranges for different revenues.

Cost should also be considered in selecting a technique. In general, a mathematically sophisticated technique is costly because it requires computer support and training. An ideal forecast technique provides acceptable accuracy with technical simplicity.

All techniques in this chapter are relatively simple and inexpensive. So, forecast accuracy is the only factor in our selection of forecast techniques. Let us use MAPE to determine the forecast accuracy of the techniques. To compute MAPE for SMA, let us consider three-year averages against actuals. The latest three-year average, for project revenue in Year 10, is ($3,907,110 + $3,766,661 + $3,281,836)/3 = $3,651,869. Then, $APE_{(Term\ 7,8,9)}$ is | $3,651,869 – $4,063,555 | /$4,063,555 = 10.13 percent. Similarly, $APE_{(Term\ 6,7,8)}$ is | $3,347,761 – $3,907,110 | /$3,907,110 = 14.32 percent, and $APE_{(Term\ 5,6,7)}$ is | $3,060,779 – $3,766,661 | /$3,766,661 = 18.74 percent. Therefore, the MAPE for SMA is (10.13 + 14.32 + 18.74)/3 = 14.40 percent. Notice that the utility revenues show an upward trend and SMA consistently underestimates them by a relatively large scale. This proves again that SMA is not an accurate tool for trend data.

We can use Excel in EXS forecasting. When a = 0.8, the APE for Year 10 is APE_{10} = | $3,856,903 – $4,063,555 | /$4,063,555 = 5.09 percent. APE_9 is | $3,656,073 – $3,907,110 | /$3,907,110 = 6.43 percent. APE_8 is | $3,213,722 – $3,766,661 | /$3,766,661 = 14.68 percent. So $MAPE_{EXS}$ is (5.09 percent + 6.43 percent + 14.68 percent)/3 = 8.73 percent.

Suppose that we consider three increments in TMA forecasting. To forecast the revenue in Year 10, we have three increments: $3,907,110 – $3,766,661 = $140,449; $3,766,661 – $3,281,836 = $484,825; and $3,281,836 – $2,994,785 = $287,051. Therefore, the forecast is $4,211,218. APE_{10} is | $4,211,218 – $4,063,555 | /$4,063,555 = 3.63 percent. Similarly, APE_9 is 3.75 percent and APE_8 is 2.08 percent. MAPE is 3.15 percent.

Table 1.7

Comparison of MAPEs

Technique	MAPE (in %)
SMA	14.40
EXS ($\alpha = 0.8$)	8.73
TMA	3.15
Regression	4.34

In regression forecasting, we can use the data of the first nine years to forecast the revenue in Year 10 and then compare it with the actual revenue in that year to get APE. Using Excel, we know that the regression equation with the data from the first nine years is revenue = \$976,464 + \$334,750 (year). The forecast revenue in Year 10 is \$976,464 + \$334,750(10) =) \$4,323,964. The APE_{10} is | \$4,323,964 − \$4,063,555 | /\$4,063,555 = 6.41 percent. APE_9 is 3.38 percent, and APE_8 is 3.24 percent. MAPE is 4.34 percent.

The MAPE comparison in Table 1.7 reveals that TMA is the most accurate forecasting tool for the utility taxes. Either TMA or regression satisfies the city benchmark of a 5 percent forecast margin.

Step 3: Forecasting

In this step, we use the selected technique, TMA, to forecast the revenue of the next year (Year 11). With three increments, the utility taxes forecast for the next year are \$4,063,555 + (\$156,445 + \$140,449 + \$484,825)/3 = \$4,324,128. We can use this figure to forecast the utility taxes in Year 12, which are \$4,324,128 + (\$260,573 + \$156,445 + \$140,449)/3 = \$4,509,950, and also forecast the revenue further into the future.

Step 4: Monitoring Forecasting Performance

The performance of a selected forecasting technique should be monitored over time. The forecast accuracy can be significantly compromised if a revenue pattern changes. In general, revenue is affected by two factors. First, socioeconomic and demographic changes can affect the size and the trend of a revenue. Second, policies or decisions regarding public service delivery and management inevitably affect revenue bases and collection capacity. A decision to increase service capacity requires enhanced revenue sources. To monitor forecast performance, we need to repeat the above three steps every year after a fiscal year ends and when the actual revenue figures become available.

Table 1.8

Revenues of the Past Five Years

Year	1	2	3	4	5
Revenues ($)	10	12	15	13	16

Exercises

1. Review Key Terms

Delphi technique
Forecast subject
Forecast horizon
Forecasting techniques
Simple moving average (SMA)
Exponential smoothing (EXS)
Smoothing constant or α
Underforecast
Overforecast
Transformation moving average (TMA)
Revenue trend
Upward trend
Downward trend
Incremental changes
Regression against time
Time-series forecasting
Quasi-causal forecasting model
Revenue predictors
Absolute percentage error (APE)
Mean absolute percentage error (MAPE)
Data outlier
Steps in revenue forecasting

2. Calculations

Table 1.8 shows the time-series data of certain revenues.

1. Use SMA, with an average of three years, to forecast the revenue in Year 6. Use your calculator to forecast, and then use Excel to confirm the result.
2. Use EXS, with $\alpha = 0.8$, to forecast the revenue in Year 6. Use your calculator to forecast, and then use Excel to confirm the result. (Note

that the Excel result is a little different from your hand calculation for the reason specified in the text, but they should be very close.)

3. Use TMA, with consideration of three increments, to forecast the revenue in Year 6. Use your calculator to forecast first, and then use Excel to confirm the result.

3. Calculations

1. The revenue from a water/sewer charge can be expressed as $T = C \times R$, where T is total annual revenue from the water/sewer charge, C is the total annual water/sewer consumption (in thousands of gallons), and R is the rate of service charge. Assuming that the total annual water/sewer consumption is 568,790 (in thousands of gallons) and the rate of the service charge is $10.50 per thousand gallons, what is total annual revenue?

2. If a revenue can be expressed as total annual forecast revenue = 10.40 + 5.50 (the year in forecast). What is the forecast revenue in Year 10? What is the forecast in Year 11? What is the difference in revenue between Year 10 and Year 11?

3. If a forecast is 35.00 and the actual figure turns out to be 40.00, what is the APE of this forecast? Suppose that another forecast of the same revenue with the same forecasting technique but different forecast periods is 46.00, and the actual figure is 42.00, what is the APE for this second forecast? What is the MAPE for the above two forecasts?

4. Forecasting Licenses, Permits, and Fees in the City of Sun Lake, California

Table 1.9 presents the historical information of licenses, permits, and fees in the city of Sun Lake, California.

1. Use SMA (from the receipts of the last three years), EXS, and TMA (consider three incremental changes for your computation) to forecast the revenue in Year 8.

2. If we know that the receipt of licenses, permits, and fees in Year 8 was $23,210,218, which of the above forecasting techniques is most accurate?

3. Use the most accurate method to forecast the receipts of licenses, permits, and fees in Years 9, 10, and 11. Use the Year 8 actual figure

Table 1.9

Licenses, Permits, and Fees in Sun Lake

Year	Revenues ($)
1	13,717,979
2	14,369,907
3	16,232,768
4	15,693,711
5	17,684,099
6	18,276,037
7	20,289,136
8	?

Table 1.10

Franchise Taxes in Sunbelt

Year	Revenues ($)
1	12,442,000
2	12,427,000
3	13,091,000
4	13,743,000
5	14,306,000
6	15,089,000
7	15,257,000
8	16,749,000
9	17,655,000

instead of the forecast figure. Also consider three incremental changes in forecasting.

4. Use Excel to build a regression model. Use this model to forecast the receipt of licenses, permits, and fees in Year 8. Is this a more accurate method than SMA, TMA, or EXS?

5. Forecasting Franchise Tax in Sunbelt

Franchise taxes are levied on businesses that gain a franchise right of doing business in a jurisdiction's territory. The data in Table 1.10 are franchise tax revenues in the city of Sunbelt, Florida, from Year 1 to Year 9.

During forecasting, you are informed that BellSouth's (the local telephone service provider) current franchise contract with the city ends in Year 11. The city will seek a 10 percent franchise tax increase from the previous year basis from BellSouth in Year 12 (as the result of a change in the tax base). The franchise tax receipts from BellSouth during the last nine years are shown

Table 1.11

Franchise Taxes from BellSouth in Sunbelt

Year	Revenues ($)
1	3,727,000
2	4,100,000
3	3,927,000
4	4,435,000
5	5,722,000
6	6,036,000
7	5,950,000
8	6,700,000
9	7,062,000

Table 1.12

Miscellaneous Revenues

Year	Revenues ($)
1	4,250,656
2	5,138,322
3	5,188,121
4	4,555,235
5	5,151,239
6	8,968,142
7	10,742,718
8	8,249,782
9	10,783,255
10	7,556,219

in Table 1.11. Forecast the franchise tax revenues of Years 10 to 12. Write a report on your forecast.

6. Forecasting Miscellaneous Revenue

Table 1.12 shows a city's miscellaneous revenues for the last ten years. An investigation reveals that the drastic increase from Year 5 to Year 6 was due to a new reclassification of the city's "fines and forfeitures." About 20 percent of the miscellaneous revenue was not included before Year 6. Before forecast, the finance director told you that he would rather underestimate than overestimate this revenue, as overestimation leaves the city no room for spending flexibility. The director even suggested that he would take 95 percent your forecast. What is your strategy to deal with this forecasting conservatism? What is your forecast of the city's miscellaneous revenues for the next year?

7. Forecast Revenues of Your Choice

Forecast the three largest revenues from a government of your choice.

CHAPTER 2

Resource Development Analysis

Learning Objectives

After studying this chapter, you should be able to

- Define a resource development issue
- Estimate revenue shortage
- Develop revenue options
- Assess revenue options
- Determine optimal revenue options

Imagine that your city needs a new police or fire station, a new city hall, a significant increase in police patrol personnel, or a large increase in payoffs for employee sick leave. Imagine that the city loses revenues as a result of economic decline, or that a major business has decided to relocate and the city will lose a large revenue base because of the relocation. All these events cause revenue shortage and require the city to explore its financial resources to deal with the shortage. In this chapter, we study a tool to deal with revenue shortage.

Resource development analysis includes an estimate of revenue shortage—how much it will be, when it will happen, and how long it will last. It also requires an analysis of potential revenue sources to cover the shortage. As opposed to revenue forecasting, which emphasizes *how much* of the revenue is available, resource development analysis concerns not only how much revenue, but also *where* it comes from.

Concepts and the Tool

Resource development analysis (RDA) applies to a fiscal condition where a significant revenue increase or expenditure cut is needed for a large revenue shortage foreseeable in the near future. *Revenue shortage* results from one of three conditions—a significant expenditure increase, a significant revenue loss, or both.

It is important to note that RDA is necessary for large and persistent revenue shortages that could severely hinder an organization's service quality and affect its financial viability. Small, temporary, or incremental revenue shortages may be dealt with by use of financial reserves or other established financial practices, and RDA may not be necessary. For example, the shortage caused by annual employee salary raises to offset inflation can be covered by allocation of a certain percentage of the budget for the increase, and no specific justification or analysis is needed. RDA consists of several steps:

- Understanding the issue. In this step, a revenue shortage and possible causes of it are specified.
- Estimating the amount of revenue shortage.
- Developing revenue options. Possible revenue options to deal with the shortage are developed.
- Assessing revenue options. Pros and cons of each revenue option are analyzed.
- Making decisions. Finally, a decision on which revenue option(s) is most feasible is made.

It is important to note that RDA is a feasibility analysis on revenue options. RDA is a first step in budget creation, but is not a budget in itself, which requires further clarification of revenue base, structure, administration, and collections.

Defining the Issue: Revenue Shortage

Many policy and management actions have financial consequences. Efforts to improve police response may force more spending on police vehicles or transportation. Policies to increase student academic performance may lead to more expenditures to hire better teachers or improve facilities. Actions to appease resident complaints about high water rates may result in a lower rate structure that leads to less revenue from that source. Some financial consequences take the form of expenditure increases (e.g., purchase of land, building, or equipment), while others are reflected as revenue loss (e.g., water rate cut). Regardless of the form of consequences, they eventually lead to a common fiscal phenomenon—revenue shortage, which can be broadly defined as: The Amount of Expenditure (or Expense) – The Amount of Revenue.

The amount of shortage (Expenditure – Revenue) can be measured by its relative size to the total revenue (or expenditure). For example, if the shortage is $1 million of $100 million revenue, the shortage is 1 percent (1/100). Another measure of shortage is the percentage of the shortage in financial reserve. A large and continual revenue shortage is a financial warning sign and necessitates an RDA.

Revenue shortage is the result of revenue loss, expenditure growth, or both. Causes of revenue shortage are many. First, changes in socioeconomic environments may cause the shortage. Population increase, especially if it is rapid, could create high demand for services and therefore rapid expenditure growth. Population decline could erode the revenue base and result in revenue loss. Economic depression could cause a loss of revenues that rely on economic growth and property valuation. Second, policy changes could also lead to a significant decline in revenues or increase in expenditures. A decision to put more police officers on the street will surely increase police expenditures. Building a new fire station increases expenditures significantly. Infrastructure improvement and maintenance are other reasons of significant expenditure increase. A decision to annex a neighborhood can cause expenditure growth in the area. Third, large and unexpected events could also drive up expenditures or reduce revenues. The damage from natural disasters such as hurricanes could leave a financial hole amounting to billions, so could man-made disasters such as terrorist attacks. Most of these events cause both an unexpected expenditure climb and revenue loss.

Some shortages are short term and one time. Others are long lasting. A shortage caused by tourist decline due to a major hurricane may last a couple of weeks, while loss of a major business taxpayer could cause a revenue shortage that lasts for years.

Estimating Revenue Shortage

Estimating revenue shortage is the most critical part of RDA because all other steps in RDA depend on it. It is also the most technically challenging because of the uncertainty involved in the estimate. Accuracy of estimation is influenced by three factors—availability of data necessary for the estimate, integrity of the existing data collection system, and assumptions made for the estimation. An accurate estimate requires that data are available, that the data collection system provides reliable data, and that the assumptions made for the estimate are proper. The ultimate purpose of the estimation is to minimize the estimation error, defined as the difference between the estimated shortage and actual shortage: Estimation Error = (Estimated Shortage − Actual Shortage)/Actual Shortage.

A negative estimation error indicates an underestimate of the shortage, and a positive sign suggests an overestimate. For example, if the estimated shortage is $5 million and the actual shortage is $6 million, then the estimate error of this underestimate is −16.67 percent ((5 − 6)/6). It is an intuitive belief that an underestimate of revenue shortage is more damaging than an overestimate because underestimates leave little room for revenue maneuvering.

There are three integrated elements in revenue shortage estimation. They are estimations of *shortage types,* the *shortage amount,* and the *time frame of shortage.* Shortage types include revenue loss, expenditure growth, or both. The shortage amount concerns the size of the shortage. The time frame of shortage concerns how long the shortage lasts. Thus, a complete estimate of revenue shortage can be phrased as, for example, "there will be a $250,000 revenue shortage for the next fiscal year as a result of hiring additional personnel." When the type and time frame of shortage are determined, estimating the shortage amount is key. The following section presents the methods of estimation. Because revenue shortage is the result of revenue loss, expenditure growth, or both, these methods are accordingly classified as methods of "estimating revenue loss" and methods of "estimating expenditure growth."

Estimating Revenue Loss

Revenue loss is the amount of revenue decline between two fiscal periods. For example, if $500 is collected this year and only $400 is available for the next year, the revenue loss is $100. Revenue loss can be broadly defined as Revenue Amount Before the Loss – Revenue Amount After the Loss.

Revenue loss occurs when the result of the above calculation is positive. In the above equation, revenue amount can be simply displayed as a function of revenue base and revenue rate (Revenue Amount = Revenue Base × Revenue Rate).

Thus, revenue loss is the result of revenue base loss, or a revenue rate cut, or both. Revenue base is the source of the revenue. For example, a local property tax base is the assessed value of properties. A retail sales tax base can be the retail sales value. The base of a utility charge could be the amount of utility consumption.

Revenue base loss can be the contributing factor to revenue loss. For example, in a city where the sales values are forecast to decline by 5 percent in one year, the revenue decline is also 5 percent when the sales tax rate is unchanged. If the expenditure level is also kept unchanged, the city will have a revenue shortage equal to 5 percent of its total sales taxes in one year.

A *revenue rate* cut can also cause a revenue shortage. The structure of the revenue rate can be flat or block. A *flat rate* means the same rate is applied regardless of the revenue amount. For example, a retail sales tax applies the same tax rate to all taxable sales regardless of the value of each sale. A *block rate* structure can be progressive or regressive. A progressive rate increases with larger revenue amounts (or higher revenue blocks), while a regressive rate increases with smaller revenue amounts (or lower revenue blocks). For example, the federal personal income tax rate has a progressive rate structure because taxpayers with higher incomes pay a higher rate.

The impact of a cut in a flat rate on revenue loss can be estimated relatively easily. For example, a 10 percent rate cut will transform to the same percent of revenue loss if the revenue base is unchanged. But for a block rate cut, revenue loss for each block (each rate bracket) of revenue must be estimated, which can be a tedious task. Statistical estimation may be used.

Let us look at an example to illustrate the estimation process. For a revenue that has a base of $1,000.00 and a flat rate of 10 percent, what is the total revenue loss if the revenue base decreases by 7 percent and the rate is reduced to 8 percent? We know that "revenue amount before the loss" is $100.00 ($1,000.00 × 10 percent). Since the base loss is 7 percent or $70 ($1,000 × 7 percent), the new base is $930. Multiplying that by 8 percent, we get $ 74.40. This is "revenue amount after the loss." So, revenue loss = $100.00 − $74.40 = $25.60. In fact, of the $25.60 loss, the base loss accounts for $7.00 (($1,000.00 × 10 percent) − ($930.00 × 10 percent)), and the rate cut accounts for $18.60 (($930.00 × 10 percent) − ($930.00 × 8 percent)).

Estimating Expenditure Growth

Estimating Purchase Prices (or Cost). The focus of this estimation is on the purchase prices of expenditure (expense) elements such as personnel, operating, and capital outlay. For example, if a new fire station is needed in a newly annexed area in a city, the estimation should be performed on the spending to hire fire personnel, the possible construction of new fire stations, the purchase of new equipment, and operations (such as training, uniforms, and office accessories). Chapter 3 describes the technique of cost estimation for a variety of cost items.

Estimation Based on Demographics. As expenditure growth is often caused by increasing public demand for services, and public demand can be measured by population growth, population growth can be used to estimate the size of expenditure increase. For example, if we can establish that, for an increase in population of 100, the expenditure increases by $100,000 ($1,000 per resident). Then if the forecast population grows by 1,000, an increase in expenditure of $1 million is expected. Similarly, if we know that the average number of residents served by one fire station, we can forecast when we may need another station for a growing population.

Table 2.1 shows total expenditures and total population in an urban city for the past ten years. If the city wants to annex an area that has 4,000 residents this year, what is the estimated expenditure for the annexation?

Table 2.1

Example of Estimating Expenditure Growth

Year	Total expenditure ($)	Population	Expenditure per capita ($)	Expenditure per capita growth rate
Ten years ago	162,491,969	168,456	964.60	
Nine years ago	162,424,561	169,675	957.27	−0.0076
Eight years ago	173,379,035	172,019	1,007.91	0.0529
Seven years ago	185,168,296	170,780	1,084.25	0.0757
Six years ago	190,753,923	170,307	1,120.06	0.0330
Five years ago	197,103,191	173,122	1,138.52	0.0165
Four years ago	229,163,984	176,373	1,299.31	0.1412
Three years ago	229,551,667	180,462	1,272.02	−0.0210
Two years ago	261,833,073	184,639	1,418.08	0.1148
Last year	258,881,807	188,013	1,376.94	−0.0290
Average				0.0418

Note: The growth rate is the result of percentage growth over the last period. For example, the growth rate of last year over two years ago was (1,376.94 − 1,418.08)/1,418.08 = −0.0290.

Both total expenditures and population showed a general trend to increase over the last ten years. Expenditures per capita have increased from $964.64 per resident ten years ago to $1,376.94 last year, for an average annual growth of 4.18 percent (or 0.0418) over the last decade. If this growth rate continues, the city will expect to spend $1,376.94 × 1.0418 = $1,434.50 per resident this year. So the total expenditures for annexation of 4,000 residents this year would be $1,434.50 × 4,000 = $5,738,000.

Other demographics, such as income, educational level, and business/residential composition of population, may also be used to estimate the growth for certain types of expenditures. For example, a highly educated population may suggest a strong need for expenditure growth on certain amenities such as community libraries.

Estimation Based on Comparable Scenarios. This method is particularly useful when little reliable information on purchase prices or demographics is available. The essence of the method is the development of comparable spending scenarios. If a city wants to construct and operate a community park, the expenditures of existing parks can be used in the estimate. If a city wants to operate an emergency management service (EMS), it can use EMS expenditures of similar cities as an estimation basis. The following example illustrates a simple process of estimation.

Table 2.2

Two Possible Spending Scenarios

	City A	City B
Total expenditure ($)	17,911,569	2,539,480
Population	38,349	42,738
Expenditure per capita ($)	467.08	527.39

Suppose that Community X (population estimate 35,000) wants to know the total expenditure of becoming incorporated (becoming a city). It has selected two recently incorporated cities (City A and City B) in developing spending scenarios. These two cities are comparable to Community X because they are all located in the same geographical region, they are all mainly residential areas, and they have similar socioeconomic characteristics in residential income and population. These two cities also provide a list of services that Community X intends to provide. The annual spending level of these two cities is shown in Table 2.2.

If Community X wanted to become City A, the estimated expenditure would be $467.08 \times 35,000 = \$16,347,800$. If it were to become City B, the estimate would be $527.39 \times 35,000 = \$18,458,650$.

Notice that this scenario method involves several critical assumptions. Mainly, it assumes the compared entities provide similar services, and have similar demographics. Violation of these assumptions leads to an inaccurate estimate.

Developing Revenue Options

Once the amount of revenue shortage is determined, potential sources should be identified to cover the shortage. A common strategy to deal with revenue shortage is to cut spending. Spending cuts can effectively reduce revenue shortage. Nevertheless, it will affect services and people. Also, it is often politically risky for public officials. The persistent multiple-year spending cut is particularly difficult, making it impossible to be used as a long-term strategy to deal with revenue shortage. In this section, we only look into options of revenue increase.

The choice of revenues to cover a revenue shortage depends on the *applicability* of these revenues to the shortage. This section briefly introduces revenue options and their applicability to cover a revenue shortage. This book is not intended to explain the design detail of each revenue option, which is part of almost any public budgeting textbook.

Option 1: Increasing Taxes

If the revenue shortage is caused by tax revenue loss or expenditure increase in supporting *governmental activities,* the shortage can be covered by a tax increase. Governmental activities are those that private businesses by themselves fail to provide in sufficient quantity or quality. Examples of governmental activities include public safety, education, and interstate highway transportation. The term "governmental activities" is used to distinguish them from business-type activities such as provision of utilities, though both can be provided by a governmental agency.

Both the tax base and the tax rate can be raised. To increase the tax base, there should be a process of redefining or reassessing the tax base. For example, the tax base of the retail sales tax could be broadened to include more previously exempt items. The same could be done to the personal income tax. A different choice of assessment methods can increase the assessed value to collect more property taxes. Technically, raising a tax rate may be easier than redefining the tax base. Local property tax rates change often. Nevertheless, for a large revenue shortage, small and incremental adjustment of the tax rate may not be enough. Change of the tax base or developing new taxes may be necessary.

If increasing existing taxes is not enough to cover the shortage, the establishment of a new tax can be considered. However, the development of a new tax requires more work than the adjustment of existing taxes. Establishment of a new tax can be very costly economically, politically, and legally. The tax law would need to be approved through a referendum. Additionally, the tax base and tax rate need to be defined, and the tax collection and enforcement processes need to be established.

Option 2: Increasing User Charges

If the revenue shortage is caused by the provision of business-type services, user charges should be considered. *Business-type services (activities)* are those that can be exchanged in the market and a price structure can be established for providers to at least break even. Provision of public utilities such as water treatment and electricity is an example. Other examples include charges for use of public highways (toll roads), and charges for using public infrastructures.

A revenue design for user charges is similar to a tax design in that it has a revenue base and revenue rate (i.e., The Revenue Amount = Revenue Base × Revenue Rate). For example, a water charge has the following design elements: The Amount of Water Charge = Water Consumption × Charge Rate.

Therefore, an increase in either the base or the rate will bring in more revenues. One advantage of user charges, compared with taxes, is that the payer benefits directly and proportionally from the service supported by the charge. With taxes, taxpayers often do not benefit directly and/or proportionally from tax-supported services. Because of this, user charges are considered fair, and perhaps more acceptable to the public than taxes. Therefore, if either is considered applicable to a revenue shortage, a user charge may be a more feasible and politically acceptable choice.

Option 3: Borrowing

In U.S. state and local governments, borrowing is desirable when the revenue shortage is caused by an increase in purchasing durable capital assets such as real estate and equipment. These capital items often have large price tags and long, useful lives.

Once debt is issued to purchase a capital asset, the payoff of the principal and interest can be matched to the life of the asset so payers (residents) can pay as they use or benefit from the capital asset. Therefore, borrowing is considered a financing method fair to taxpayers.

Bonds can be issued to deal with revenue shortage in governmental activities and business-type activities. Once a bond is issued to finance governmental activities, it is often supported by the taxing authority, which means that the repayment of principal and interest is assured by taxing power. This means that the bond buyer has a claim on the taxes of the issuing unit equal to their investment in its bonds. Such assurance may not exist for a bond issued for business-type activities, which can be repaid from the revenue generated by the activities. The former is called "full-faith-and-credit" (or "general obligation") debt, while the latter is called "nonguaranteed" debt (or a "revenue" bond).

Option 4: Intergovernmental Assistance

Intergovernmental assistance is often in the form of grants and revenue (or tax) sharing. For local governments, federal grants are sources of revenue to cover revenue shortages in areas specified by the federal government. Large and popular federal grants are in the areas of public safety, economic development, health and social services, job training, education, and public mass transportation. Federal fiscal support may also be available during emergencies or natural disasters such as hurricanes and earthquakes. States also provide grants to local governments in their jurisdictions. Although intergovernmental assistance is considered an applicable source of revenue in case of revenue shortage, strict requirements are often associated with acquisition of grants. Uncertainty is involved in acquiring grants and in their continuation. For example, there is always a time lag between applying for a grant and receiving it. Also, many grants for local governments provide funds only for new rather than existing services/programs. Many other grants need matched funds from receiving governments. All these limitations make intergovernmental assistance less attractive than some other revenue sources to cover revenue shortage.

Option 5: Use of Financial Reserves

A financial reserve is the accumulated result of a desirable difference between revenues and expenditures (i.e., revenues > expenditures). Continuation of this difference over a long period of time can accumulate a large amount of financial resources available to be used in the case of revenue shortage. The use of financial reserve is always one of the first options to cover revenue shortage. Nevertheless, if the shortage is long and large, the existing financial reserve will eventually be depleted and other options will have to be considered.

Option 6: Making Institutional or Policy Changes

Any institutional change may have a financial impact. One policy that has been used to deal with revenue shortage at the local level is to develop economic incentive packages to attract business in order to enlarge the revenue base. Besides, efforts in outsourcing and contracting out may reduce expenditures and indirectly help reduce revenue shortages. Nevertheless, institutional changes often take years to have any significant effect, and the impact of these changes on revenue shortage is likely to be long term.

Option 7: Combination of the Above Options and a Summary

An organization is likely to use more than one option in dealing with revenue shortage. This approach is particularly useful for a large revenue shortage, or for a new community that starts levying its own revenues. Tables 2.3 and 2.4 present a summary, based on the applicability of the above options to address revenue shortage.

Assessing Revenue Options

Developing revenue options is the first step in assessing the feasibility of revenue options to cover revenue shortage. Once revenue options are considered applicable, they should be assessed to select the optimal revenue option

Table 2.3

Applicability of Revenue Options According to Activity Type

	Revenue shortage caused by	
	Governmental activities	Business-type activities
Taxes	Applicable	Not applicable
User charges	Not applicable	Applicable
Borrowing	Applicable	Applicable
Intergovernmental aids	Applicable	Questionable
Financial reserves	Applicable	Applicable
Institutional/policy changes	Applicable	Applicable

Table 2.4

Applicability of Revenue Options According to Time Frame

	Revenue shortage is	
	Short term (< 3 years)	Long term (≥ 3 years)
Taxes	Applicable	Applicable
User charges	Applicable	Applicable
Borrowing	Questionable	Applicable
Intergovernmental aids	Applicable	Not applicable
Financial reserves	Applicable	Not applicable
Institutional/policy changes	Not applicable	Applicable

(or options). If possible, always prepare multiple revenue options for the purpose of comparison. Consideration in evaluating revenue options should be placed on their financial, political, legal, and administrative merits.

In assessing *financial merit,* financial costs of options should be estimated and compared. Financial costs include costs of revenue option development (e.g., the feasibility study), revenue design (e.g., the rate study), and revenue administration and collection (e.g., registration, assessment, accounting, delinquency control/compliance, audit, appeal, and enforcement). The revenue amount should be estimated to determine whether enough revenue can be generated from an option. The *revenue to cost ratio,* which represents the revenue generated for each dollar of cost (Revenue Generated/Cost), can be used to assess the cost-effectiveness of a revenue option in generating resources. A higher ratio indicates a more financially efficient revenue option.

The *political merit* of revenue options concerns whether and how much political support exists for a revenue option. Although a revenue option may have high financial merit, lack of popular or political support may make it impossible to be implemented. There are plenty of cases in which proposals for tax increases live only to be rejected by citizens or elected officials. To estimate and understand the level of political support for a revenue option, an assessment of the possible impact of the option on each governmental stakeholder (i.e., citizens, elected officials, businesses, and other interest groups) is needed.

In addition to political feasibility, there are *legal and regulatory requirements* associated with development of revenue options. The law may set limits on tax rate, tax base, and tax exemptions and deductions. The level of legal compliance related to each revenue option should be assessed. Legal or regulatory requirements may be placed on a grantee government in order to receive intergovernmental assistance.

Making Decisions

After assessment, a decision should be made to select a revenue option or options that are the most feasible. A *decision-making matrix* can be used to select the best option or options. The matrix specifies a list of criteria to be used to evaluate merits of each revenue option. In creating the matrix, each evaluation criterion is assessed and assigned a numeric score for each revenue option. The scores of all criteria are added to arrive at a total score for an option, which can be used to determine the most feasible option. Table 2.5 presents a simplified example of the matrix, with three revenue options being evaluated. More items in each category of financial, political, or legal merits can be added (or eliminated) to fit evaluation requirements and conditions of each case.

In the case where only a single revenue option is evaluated, the total numeric score can be used as a reference in comparison with an acceptable score. A value higher than that score indicates the option is acceptable. For example, on a scale system with 1 being extremely unfeasible and 10 being extremely feasible, a score of 5 may indicate moderate feasibility. Therefore, a revenue option scoring higher than the average score of 5 should be considered acceptable.

A Case Study

Woodbury is a residential community located in an unincorporated area in Greenfield County, Florida, which is a county of 1,130,367 residents. Woodbury's 8,000 residents rely on the county for general government, police, parks and recreation, environment management (pollution control, environmental protection, and natural resource conservation), and local transportation (local road construction and maintenance, traffic engineering, and street lighting). Woodbury's community association has a budgeted

Table 2.5

The Decision-Making Matrix for Revenue Options

Ratings: 0 = Extremely unfeasible. . . . .10 = Extremely feasible

	Options		
	1	2	3
Financial Merits			
Cost of the feasibility study			
Cost of the revenue design study			
Cost of administration and collection			
Sufficiency of revenue generated			
Revenue/cost ratio			
Political Merits			
Elected officials' acceptance			
General public's acceptance			
Business community's acceptance			
Other interest groups' acceptance			
Legal Feasibility			
Compliance with federal legal requirements			
Compliance with state legal requirements			
Compliance with local legal requirements			
Total score			

expenditure of $3,680,373 this year, with major spending in administrative services ($1,710,737), community landscaping and maintenance ($1,305,078), recreation activities ($199,232), and publication of a community monthly journal and several newsletters ($71,521).

Woodbury is considered an affluent community in the county. A recent issue of *Realtor Today* reports that the median value of residential single-family homes in Woodbury is $199,000, compared with $176,000 countywide. Many Woodbury residents believe their community pays more in taxes than they receive in services from the county. These residents are the force behind a movement to seek alternative service providers. Woodbury is bordered by Summertown, a city of 196,235 people, that has a reputation for its beauty and amiable weather all year long. Summertown has long courted Woodbury to leave the county and become part of the city. Summertown's most recent proposal to Woodbury includes a package that likely would freeze the property tax rate for Woodbury residents for three years.

Many officials in Greenfield County are very concerned. They are afraid that if Woodbury incorporates or is annexed, the county will lose a large revenue base. Worse, other wealthy unincorporated areas in the county could follow suit in leaving the county. Steve Loveless, a senior financial analyst for the county, offered to perform an analysis on the potential revenue loss for the county if Woodbury leaves.

Step 1: Defining the Issue

Steve thought that, although Woodbury might generate a large amount of revenue for the county, the county also spends a lot of money in the area. Therefore, it is still not clear if the county will lose money if Woodbury leaves. If Woodbury is a net revenue generator for the county, its leaving will cause the county a revenue shortage. So, the first question in the analysis is whether or not there will be a revenue shortage for the county as the result of Woodbury's leaving. To answer this question, Steve needs to estimate the expenditure by the county in Woodbury and the revenue generated from the area. If a revenue shortage would occur, the size of it will be estimated in the analysis. Finally, an analysis should be conducted to explore potential revenue options for covering the revenue shortage, if it will occur.

Step 2: Estimating Revenue Shortage

How Much Can the County Save in Expenditure
If Woodbury Leaves?

How much does the county spend in Woodbury? The county provides Woodbury with public services. Private contractors provide water and sewer services and garbage/solid waste management so these services are excluded in the county's analysis. Woodbury will stay in its current fire and rescue and emergency management services district in the county even after it leaves, so no expenditure saving is expected from this service for the county.

Steve assumed that Woodbury would make the annexation decision next year, and he also used a ten-year period in his projection of expenditure saving and revenue loss. In estimation, Steve first calculated a population percentage of Woodbury in the county (8,000/1,130,367 = 0.71 percent). Then he derived the county's spending in Woodbury by multiplying this percentage with the county's forecast expenditures for next year in general government, law enforcement, culture and recreation, environmental management, and local transportation.

Steve realized that using population proportion might not be accurate for local transportation. Woodbury has forty-three miles of paved roadway, about 2.35 percent of the county total. Using this measure, Steven adjusted the county's spending for transportation in Woodbury ($87,124,143 × 2.35 percent) as $2,047,417. Also, the county has a park in Woodbury. Steve

Table 2.6

Estimated Expenditure Next Year in Woodbury ($)

	Greenfield County	Woodbury estimate by population percentage	Adjusted Woodbury estimate
General government	178,523,456	1,263,473	1,263,473
Police	372,252,665	2,634,561	2,634,561
Parks and recreation	44,276,096	313,357	1,275,152
Environment management	39,145,829	277,049	277,049
Transportation	87,124,143	616,608	2,047,417
Total	721,322,189	5,105,048	7,497,652

was able to calculate the county's spending on the park ($753,456), plus an estimate of expenditures for other recreation activities ($521,696), and therefore estimated that the county would spend about $1,275,152 total on "Parks and Recreation" in Woodbury. After these adjustments, Steve created Table 2.6. The figures in the last column represent his estimate of county spending in Woodbury.

The estimate shows that the county will spend $7,497,652 in Woodbury next year. But, if Woodbury left, would the county be able to save all of this money? Probably not in the short term. For example, it would be difficult to cut the spending on county personnel even if Woodbury leaves. Some members of the workforce might be reassigned to other areas. But much of the savings from personnel would have to come from long-term labor force attrition or early retirement buyouts. Also, in the short term, it would be impossible to eliminate the spending on capital outlay (building, land, and durable equipment) that has already been purchased. Therefore, the short-term saving from Woodbury's leaving would most likely come from a reduction in operating expenses such as office supplies, utility overhead, inexpensive office equipment, and other operating expenditures related to Woodbury. In the county's operating budget this year, only 20 percent is for operating expenses, so Steve estimated, if Woodbury leaves next year, the county will likely save 20 percent of the $7,497,652, which is $1,499,530. (A detailed discussion on how to calculate the expenditure change due to a policy or managerial decision can be seen in Chapter 5, "Incremental Cost Analysis".)

Nevertheless, the savings can grow over time for the next ten years to $7,497,652 at the end of the period if the county can cut its Woodbury-related personnel and capital outlay by 10 percent every year. Ten years is the average maturity of the county's current bonds, while 10 percent is an estimate from the county Human Resources office on the attrition rate of the

Table 2.7

Expenditure Saving Estimate If Woodbury Leaves

Year	Expenditure saving ($)
1 (next year)	1,499,530
2	2,249,296
3	2,999,061
4	3,748,826
5	4,498,591
6	5,248,356
7	5,998,122
8	6,747,887
9	7,497,652
10	7,497,652
Total	47,984,973

Woodbury-related workforce. Table 2.7 demonstrates the savings over a ten-year period.

How Much Revenue Does the County Lose If Woodbury Leaves?

The county collects property taxes and utility taxes from Woodbury. The county also gathers state intergovernmental assistance for Woodbury. The real property taxes are estimated from the formula Tax Amount = Total Taxable Value × Tax Rate × 95 Percent Collection Factor. Woodbury's total taxable value is $2,207,839,560 next year. The tax rate is 0.21234 percent (or the millage = 2.1234). Assume that only 95 percent of all taxes levied are eventually collected. The estimated property tax revenue next year in Woodbury is $2,207,839,560 × 0.21234 percent × 95 percent = $4,453,720.

Utility taxes are levied on the consumption of public utilities that often include electricity, water, and communication services. It is estimated that annual utility taxes per household in Woodbury are $289 next year. There are about 2,500 households in Woodbury. The estimated utility taxes are $289 × 2,500 households = $722,500 next year.

There are two types of intergovernmental revenues that the county collects for Woodbury: the retail sales tax and the local option gas tax. Both are state revenue sharing based on the population of an area. If Woodbury leaves, the county will lose population and its intergovernmental revenue will be proportionally reduced. It is estimated that the county will collect about $3,049,880 from Woodbury next year. This is the amount the county will lose if Woodbury leaves.

The total revenue collected by the county from Woodbury is estimated at $4,453,720 + $722,500 + $3,049,880 = $8,226,100 for the next year. Since it

Table 2.8

Revenue Shortage Estimate If Woodbury Leaves ($)

Year	Expenditure saving	Revenue loss	Revenue shortage
1 (next year)	1,499,530	8,226,100	−6,726,570
2	2,249,296	8,472,883	−6,223,587
3	2,999,061	8,727,069	−5,728,009
4	3,748,826	8,988,882	−5,240,056
5	4,498,591	9,258,548	−4,759,957
6	5,248,356	9,536,304	−4,287,948
7	5,998,122	9,822,394	−3,824,272
8	6,747,887	10,117,065	−3,369,179
9	7,497,652	10,420,577	−2,922,925
10	7,497,652	10,733,195	−3,235,543
Total	47,984,973	94,303,018	−46,318,045

is very likely that Woodbury's population and property values will grow about 3 percent every year for the next decade, this growth has to be used in estimating Woodbury's revenue after the next year. For example, if Woodbury leaves, the county's revenue loss would be $8,226,100 × 1.03 = $8,472,883 in two years. A ten-year estimate of the county's revenue loss is given in Table 2.8.

The amount of revenue shortage is the difference between spending saving and revenue loss. The negative sign indicates a shortage. The result indicates that, if Woodbury leaves the county, the county will lose $6.7 million next year, but the loss declines over the ten-year period. The total loss for the next ten years is more than $46 million.

Step 3: Developing Revenue Options

Steve presented the findings to the county administration and commission. A grim picture of an annual revenue shortage of $2.9 to $6.7 million concerned officials. The first option seemed to be to persuade Woodbury to stay by presenting an incentive package similar to the one from Summertown. However, the concern was the domino effect, that if the county did this for Woodbury, it would have to do it for other communities in the county, which could cost the county even more.

A large spending cut is hardly a choice for a county that has already faced service quality fluctuations and many citizen complaints. So the county has to explore its revenue potentials. The county relies on two major revenue sources: taxes and user charges. County taxes include property taxes, utility taxes, sales taxes (shared with the state and other local governments), local option gas taxes (shared with the state and other local governments), and tourist development taxes (levied on tourist-related industries such as hotels, restaurants, and shops). The county's user charges include water/sewer treatment charges to some customers that use the county's treatment facilities, and charges for the use of the county's convention center.

Since the revenue shortage would mainly occur in governmental activities (the county mainly provides governmental services to Woodbury), any increase in user charges was ruled out. Of the major tax revenues, the county's share of sales taxes and local option gas taxes was predetermined by the state, based on an established revenue-sharing formula. Unless the county had a referendum to increase the tax rate on the top of the current rate, these two taxes should be excluded as revenue options to cover the shortage. Therefore, the only options left are to increase in property taxes, utility taxes, and tourist development taxes.

Step 4: Assessing Revenue Options

Utility taxes generate about 5 percent of total county tax revenues. It will have to take a significant increase (4.2 percent) to generate enough revenue to cover the shortage. The utility tax rate in the county is considered one of the highest in the state. A rate hike will meet substantial resistance from utility businesses and customers. Also, a higher rate may curb utility consumption, which will eventually offset the revenue increase. After careful consideration, the utility tax rate increase is ruled out.

The county property tax rate is considered moderate in the state. Because the total assessed value has increased over the last decade, the county has been able to reduce the tax rate over years. So, in theory, there is a potential for an increase in the property tax rate. Also, the collection cost is negligible for such an increase, as the administrative process already exists. A calculation shows that a rate increase of 1.35 percent should bring the county an additional $7 million, which is enough to cover the revenue shortage. Nevertheless, such an increase is considered significant and may face a political challenge from residents. A substantial amount of persuasion may be needed.

Another resort is the tourist development taxes. Since the taxes are levied on a limited number of businesses, a rate increase is unlikely to face heavy resistance from residents. Nevertheless, these businesses already pay a higher rate than others. A rate increase on top of the current high rate could cause some businesses to close down, which would reduce the revenue due to a smaller tax base. Word is out that the tourist industry is lobbying the county commission to eliminate or reduce the current tourist development taxes. Three (out of seven) commissioners from the county's business-heavy districts are likely to support such a proposal. They only need one more vote to deter any effort to increase these taxes.

Step 5: Making Decisions

The final analysis indicates that a rate increase in property taxes is the most likely revenue option. Steve estimated that the rate increase as the result of Woodbury's leaving would likely range from 1.350 percent next year to 0.054 percent ten years later. However, the scope of this rate increase is restricted by the state law and depends on the assessed property value of the county, which is expected to grow about 3 percent annually during the next decade. If such growth ceases to exist, the county then needs a larger rate increase. Three weeks after Steve presented his report, three hurricanes struck his county and the damage to the property was immeasurable. Steve was forced to readjust his analysis.

Exercises

1. Review Key Terms

Resource development analysis (RDA)
Revenue shortage
Steps in RDA
Elements in revenue shortage estimation
Revenue loss
Revenue base
Revenue rate
Flat rate
Block rate
Purchase price estimation of expenditure growth
Demographics estimation of expenditure growth
Comparable scenarios estimation of expenditure growth
Increasing taxes as a revenue option
Increasing user charges as a revenue option
User charge design (a revenue design for user charges)
Borrowing as a revenue option
Intergovernmental assistance as a revenue option
Use of financial reserves as a revenue option
Institutional/policy changes as a revenue option
Applicability of revenue options for activity type
Applicability of revenue options for time frame

Table 2.9

A Sales Tax Example

	This year	Next year
Retail sales value ($)	23,902,346	24,567,390
Exemption ($)	12,345,670	16,345,670
Tax rate (%)	7.5	7.5

Table 2.10

A User Charge Example

Consumption block (gallons)	Rate (per 1,000 gallons)	Consumption this year (gallons)	Consumption next year (gallons)
0 to 3,000	$7.08	243,578,500	231,349,400
Above 3,000	$9.54	124,760,340	100,760,350

Revenue/cost ratio
Financial, political, legal, and administrative merits of a revenue option
Decision-making matrix

2. Calculation

A state plans to increase the number of items exempted from its retail sales tax. The tax amount is defined as (Retail Sales Value – Exemption) × Tax Rate. Table 2.9 shows the expected change.

1. What is the revenue shortage (as the result of revenue loss) if there is any, based on the information in Table 2.9?
2. If the actual shortage is $345,291, what is the estimation error?
3. Refer to Table 2.9. If the tax rate increases from 7.5 percent this year to 8.0 percent next year and all other estimations are unchanged, what is the estimated revenue shortage, if there is any?
4. Refer to Table 2.9. If the tax rate increases from 7.5 percent this year to 8.0 percent next year and all other estimations are unchanged, and if the actual shortage is $345,291, what is the estimation error?

3. Calculation

City A is expecting a decline in its residential water/sewer user charges as a result of population decline. Table 2.10 shows the estimated consumption change.

Table 2.11

An Example of Expenditure Estimation

Year	Police expenditure ($)	Population
Ten years ago	111,575,000	443,611
Nine years ago	122,258,000	455,367
Eight years ago	131,633,000	465,895
Seven years ago	139,379,000	470,553
Six years ago	154,738,000	507,553
Five years ago	160,490,000	512,628
Four years ago	182,975,000	527,291
Three years ago	188,884,000	551,645
Two years ago	203,431,000	579,684
Last year	211,635,000	594,176

1. What is the total estimated amount of the water/sewer user charge this year?
2. What is the revenue shortage of this user charge as the result of the consumption decline?
3. If the actual shortage is $275,654, what is the estimation error of the shortage?

4. Calculation

Table 2.11 shows police expenditures and population figures for the past ten years. What is the estimated police expenditure per capita for the next year?

5. Application

Numerous policy and management actions have financial consequences that can lead to revenue shortage. Identify one of these actions from your local communities and perform an RDA.

CHAPTER 3

Cost Estimation

Learning Objectives

After studying this chapter, you should be able to

- Calculate total cost, average cost, direct cost, indirect cost, personnel cost, operating cost, and capital cost
- Perform cost allocation
- Use cost depreciation methods
- Apply average cost to determine efficiency

Cost is a critical concept in the private sector. It helps calculate profit, which is the difference between cost and revenue. Cost has limited use in many public agencies because profitability is not the goal of their operations. Nevertheless, cost is still important to them for several reasons.

First, many public service agencies, including public and nonprofit agencies, provide goods that can be exchanged in the market. Examples include garbage collection, toll transportation, water and sewer treatments and supply, and other utility supply. The production of these goods requires a *breakeven* (i.e., revenue = cost), and production is inefficient and not viable if a breakeven or profit is not achieved. Second, cost provides a measure of efficiency—how well a resource is spent to produce a product. Cost helps managers determine whether the use of a resource is maximized and waste is avoided. Cost also interests stakeholders, such as elected officials, and private citizens who pay for services. Third, the increasing use of performance-based budgeting requires availability of performance measures that includes cost measures. In a performance-based budgeting, decision makers use cost information to assess program efficiency and make resource allocation decisions. Finally, cost is a useful standard in making privatization or outsourcing decisions. Advocates of privatization have cited the case of inefficient operations in the public sector in their argument for contracting out public services to the private sector. Part of the argument is that a service should be produced by a sector that is more efficient in using resources. Therefore, the selection of service providers should be based partly on cost.

Concepts and the Tool

Cost is different from expenditure or expense. The terms *expenditure* or *expense* are often associated with the budget cycle, as in "expenditures of the police department for *this fiscal year.*" These terms convey a clear sense of the annual or biennial time frame of a budget cycle. Cost is not necessarily a budget concept. It does not have to be associated with a particular fiscal period. Strictly speaking, cost is resource consumption of a product, service, program, or process for a given time frame.

Cost and expenditure may be different in dollar amounts. Expenditure is the amount of money spent during a fiscal cycle. However, money spent does not necessarily translate into cost. For example, the amount spent to purchase an expensive computer system is the expenditure during the year of the purchase. If the computer is used for more than one year, only part of the expenditure should be counted as cost for the year of the purchase.

Two concepts are important for cost estimation: cost objective and cost time frame. *Cost objective* concerns the cost of "what." It can be a program, project, process, or function. A well-defined cost objective is critical for cost estimation. *Cost time frame* concerns the time period for which the estimation is made: lifetime of a program, annual estimation, or biennial estimation. Both cost objective and cost time frame should be determined prior to cost estimation.

Cost Classification

Total Cost and Average Cost

Cost is the resource consumed to produce a product or a service. For example, to provide a police patrol in a community, patrol officers have to be paid and provided with patrol vehicles and necessary equipment. The payments for police salaries, vehicles, and weapons are called *cost items* (or *cost elements*). They are resources consumed to produce a product, in this case, police patrol. *Total cost* (also called *full cost*) is the dollar value of all related cost items that should be assigned to a cost objective. Although this concept is relatively clear, calculating total cost is rather difficult in the real world. Complete accuracy is almost impossible to achieve for most public services. In most cases of cost estimation, assumptions have to be made on the time frame of a cost objective, on inclusion (or exclusion) of cost items, and on distribution of certain cost items. We will come back to this point later in this chapter.

If we know the total cost of a police patrol program, and we also know the total number of patrols conducted, we can compute cost per patrol. This measure is called *average cost* (or *unit cost*).

$$\text{Average Cost} = \text{Total Cost/Quantity}$$

In this equation, quantity (also called "volume") is a measure of the output of a product or service. Examples of average cost include "cost of making a police arrest," "cost of providing a gallon of water," or "cost of providing elementary education to one student."

Average cost allows us to compare efficiency. For example, we can compare the average cost of two elementary schools. Let us say School A has 500 students with an annual cost of $5 million, and School B has 1,000 students with an annual cost of $7 million. The average cost is $10,000 per student ($5 million/500 students) for School A, and $7,000 per student ($7 million/ 1,000 students) for School B. We can say that School B is more efficient than School A in this measure.

Why is average cost a measure of efficiency? Notice that, in the above example, it tells us how much a school spends on each student. We say School B is more efficient because it consumes less to educate a student.

Direct Cost and Indirect Cost

Some cost items can be directly assigned to a cost objective. For example, the salary of a police officer in a local police department is a *direct cost* to the department. *Indirect cost* cannot be directly assigned to a cost objective. It should be allocated to it in some manner. One example is a city manager's salary as a cost of the police department. Although the manager is not involved in the daily operation of the department, he or she does contribute to the planning and management of the department. So the city manager's salary is an indirect cost item of the police department and should be distributed to its cost in an indirect fashion.

The process of distributing cost to goods or services is referred to as *cost allocation.* Let us look at a simple example to illustrate this process. Suppose that the total cost of a purchasing department is $25,000 this year, and we need to allocate this cost to two service departments: Public Safety and Public Utilities. Let us say that the purchasing department issues a total of 500 purchase orders (POs) this year. So, the cost per PO is $25,000/500 = $50. In cost allocation, this is called the *overhead rate.* The $25,000 is the *cost pool,* which is the cost that needs to be allocated. The 500 POs, or "the number of POs issued," is the *cost base.* Cost base is a very important concept in costing. It is a measure of an activity that incurs the cost. Later in this chapter, we will show that the choice of cost base largely determines the cost allocated to a program. The above example illustrates that overhead rate is determined as follows:

$$\text{Overhead Rate} = \text{Cost Pool/Cost Base}$$

Let us say that, of the 500 POs issued, 300 are for Public Safety and 200 for Public Utilities. The cost allocated to Public Safety is $50 \times 300 = \$15,000$. Similarly, the cost for Public Utilities is $50 \times 200 = \$10,000$. That is

$$\text{Cost Allocated to a Program} = \text{Overhead Rate} \times$$
$$\text{Cost Base Shared by the Program}$$

The complexity of cost allocation methods varies. Some methods, such as activity-based costing, can be quite complicated. *Activity-based costing* (ABC) is a method of cost allocation that emphasizes allocation precision. It requires careful study of the process and activities that incur costs so that a cause–effect relationship can be established between costs and activities. In the above example, some purchases consume more resources than others do (the purchase of expensive policing equipment is much more complex than the purchase of simple office stationery). In ABC, the actual resource consumption of the purchasing department for each service department is measured and used to distribute the cost of the purchasing department.

Personnel Cost, Operating Cost, Capital Cost

Personnel cost is the cost of providing personnel services. It often includes salaries, bonuses, and fringe benefits. *Operating cost* is the cost of sustaining daily operations. Costs of office supplies are examples. *Capital cost* refers to the cost associated with acquisition of long-lived, nonrecurring, and expensive items. Examples include costs for buildings, lands, and capital equipment.

This classification helps managers in many ways. First, personnel cost is the largest cost element for many governmental agencies. Reporting it separately from other cost elements helps management track it and develop means to control it. Second, capital items are expensive and long-term in nature, and their financial impact to an agency is often more than that of an operating item. Separation of capital costs from other costs improves financial accountability of capital projects.

Total Cost Estimation

Total cost (TC) provides useful information to management. It is important for a manager to know the cost of providing a service, supporting a program, or operating a production process. Also, total cost is necessary for computing average cost. In the following section, we explain how to estimate total cost.

The key to total cost estimation is to identify all cost items related to a cost objective, and distribute them in a rational and accurate fashion. Cost items can be identified through detailing personnel, operating, and capital cost items, as discussed in the following section.

Personnel Costs

Personnel costs of a particular program include salary, bonuses, and benefits of employees who work for the program. One way to identify personnel cost is to use an hourly rate. Consider this example: If an employee makes an annual salary and benefits of $40,000 and works a total of 2,080 hours a year, the hourly rate of salary and benefits is $40,000/2,080 = $19.23. If the employee works 400 hours annually for a particular program, then the program's annual personnel cost of this employee is $19.23 × 400 = $7,692. Realize that, in this example, the hourly rate is the overhead rate, and the 400 hours is the cost base shared by the program. To compute total personnel cost for the program, we need to include personnel costs of all employees that are involved in the program.

In this example, we use "working hours" as workload for cost allocation. Another measure is full-time equivalent (FTE), which converts working hours into a previously defined work time unit. If FTE is defined as forty work hours a week, a person who works twenty hours weekly is assigned half FTE.

Operating Costs

Operating costs support and sustain daily operations and service provisions. They may include costs associated with travel, maintenance of equipment or buildings, purchases of office supplies, acquisition of inexpensive equipment, and overhead—electricity, water, and so forth. For example, if a printer costs $500 a year to maintain (paper, toner, maintenance fees), and if it makes 1,000 copies a year and 300 of them belong to Program A, then the printing cost for Program A is $150 ($500/1,000 × 300) this year. This is a simplified example. In reality, as there are numerous operating cost items, cost allocation for all of them is a huge task (think about how many items there are in an office). So it is often a good idea to classify operating cost items into several *cost groups* and to allocate costs for these groups. Cost groups could be "stationery expenses," "equipment," and "utility expenses." For example, if an agency spends $1,000 on stationery this year, if 10 percent of the stationery is utilized by Program A, then the stationery cost for Program A is $100.

Notice that we use a "utilization" rate here to allocate the stationery cost. Determination of this utilization rate often requires careful observation, good bookkeeping practices, and accurate human judgment.

Capital Costs

These are costs for the acquisition or construction of fixed long-term assets such as buildings, land, and equipment. As capital items are used for a long time, it is necessary to spread the cost over the lifetime of these items. The effort to distribute capital cost is called *cost depreciation.* Deprecation determines the capital cost of any particular time period. There are several methods of determining capital cost deprecation, including the *straight-line* ⫟ *depreciation method* shown in this equation.

$$D = \frac{C-S}{N}$$

In the equation, D is the cost allocated during a time period, C is the cost of the asset, S is the salvage or residual value of the asset, and N is total number of time periods in the lifetime of usage. Let us say that a police vehicle is purchased for \$30,000. The vehicle will be used for five years. The residual value of the vehicle after five years is \$4,000. Therefore, the annual capital cost of the vehicle is (\$30,000 – \$4,000)/5 = \$5,200.

Realize that the straight-line method allocates the same amount (\$5,200) each year. In reality, the vehicle will perhaps be used differently over time. Suppose that it is driven more during the first three years—20,000 miles a year for the first three years and 10,000 miles a year for the remaining two years. We want to allocate cost according to the use of the vehicle—more cost for years of heavy use. How do we do that? As we know, the total cost for allocation is \$26,000 (\$30,000 – \$4,000), we also know that the number of total miles during the five years is 80,000 (20,000 miles each year for the first three years plus 10,000 miles each year for the last two years). So we know that it costs \$0.325 for a mile (\$26,000/80,000). For the 20,000 miles in the first year, the cost is \$6,500 (\$0.325 × 20,000). This depreciation method is called *usage rate,* shown in this equation.

$$D = \frac{C-S}{U} \times u$$

U is total estimated usage units during the estimated time of the asset, and u is estimated usage units during a particular time period. In this example, the annual cost for the second or the third year is \$6,500 each year. The annual cost in the fourth or fifth year is \$3,250 each year.

Average Cost Estimation

If it costs $10,000 to produce 100,000 gallons of water, the cost for each gallon is $0.10 ($10,000/100,000). If we know an elementary school spends $10,000,000 a year for 5,000 students, then the cost for each student is $2,000 ($10,000,000/5,000). Average cost (AC) is total cost (TC) divided by quantity.

Average cost is a *measure of efficiency.* It tells us the resource consumed in producing one unit of a product or service. For example, if elementary School A educates a student for $2,000 and School B does that for $1,000, we know School B is more efficient than School A in this measure. So a smaller AC indicates a more efficient production.

To calculate average cost, a measure of product quantity is needed. In the above example, it is the number of students for each school. It should be realized, though, that many governmental agencies have multiple measures of product or service quantity. For instance, instead of using the "number of students" in the above example, the "number of student credit hours" can be used. So the "average cost per student credit hour" is computed, which is also an average cost measure. It is possible that, by this measure, School A is more efficient than School B, because students in School A take more courses and have more credit hours. So, it is always a good idea to look at multiple measures to get a complete picture of efficiency when using average cost comparisons.

A Case Study

The City of Northenville (population 41,200), Illinois, is located close to a major metropolitan area in the state. The city seldom experiences serious crimes; but it has recently witnessed an increase of misdemeanor cases. Its police department has twenty-three employees, including twenty sworn officers. The police have four main functions—street patrol (including emergency response), crime investigation, internal affairs, and a community-oriented policing program (COP). The COP program was initiated two years ago, with a two-year federal grant of $500,000 ($250,000 each year). The grant expires this year and the city needs to make decision on the continuation of the program. The results of a recent program evaluation indicated the program had moderately improved citizen perception on safety; but it had no impact on crime rate.

Chief James Smith is a strong advocate for the COP program. In a recent budget preparation meeting, he argued that the program was very popular among citizens. Its elimination or cutback in any form would face citizen criticism. James suggested that the city make the effort to

renew the grant, or support it from its own financial resources. He also
stated that, since the program had already purchased its equipment in the
first year of its operation, it would cost much less than $250,000 to oper-
ate the program annually.

Edward Nortew, the finance director, disagreed. Edward pointed out that,
although the equipment purchases were made and there was no need to purchase new equipment in the next year, the equipment would be replaced
eventually. He also indicated that some communication equipment in the
COP unit was old and needed replacement very soon. He said in conclusion,
"the true cost of the program is more than $250,000. The city is going to pay
for that sooner or later."

To determine the true cost of the program and to make a budget decision
related to it, the city manager asked her management analyst, Al Stevens, to
calculate the cost of the COP. Al recently received his MPA degree and was
eager to apply his education. He first requested related information from
James and then used the following steps to develop a spreadsheet of costs.

Step 1: Determination of Personnel Costs

There are four employees currently working for the COP program—three
COP officers and a bookkeeper. An examination of COP financial records
shows that Officer A made an annual salary with benefits of $100,852 last
year. She worked 2,045 hours (including 210 overtime hours). Officer B made
$58,900 in salary and benefits last year. He worked 2,180 hours that included
100 overtime hours.

Officer C works for both the COP program and other programs in the
department. She made $68,450 in salary and benefits last year. Of a total of
2,080 hours, 832 were for COP. The bookkeeper also works for multiple
programs. Her annual salary and benefits were $40,000 for 2,080 hours last
year. It is estimated that she contributed 210 hours to COP last year. From
the information, Al calculated the personnel cost and found that COP cost
the city $191,171 in personnel last year, tallied in Table 3.1.

Step 2: Determination of Operating Costs

COP officers conduct vehicle and bike patrol in two residential communities
of the city. They also organize regular crime watch meetings with community advocates. Recently, James assigned the COP unit the responsibility of
conducting an annual citizen satisfaction survey.

Last year, the program spent $12,523 on uniform allowance and bikes,
$5,342 to organize community meetings (renting places, sending flyers, and

paying one outside speaker). COP also spent $5,000 on a citizen survey conducted by a consulting company. The items that should be allocated to the program include utilities and office/other supplies. The utility bills (telephone, water, and electricity) of the department were $5,370. The office supplies cost the department a total of $22,597.

To determine the cost base to allocate the utility bills and office supplies, Al conducted interviews with James and several other administrative officers in the city. It became clear to Al that it was almost impossible to reach a consensus on how much of the utility bills and office supplies should be allocated to COP. Al finally decided to use the "number of employees" as cost base to allocate these two items. His logic was that, since four of twenty-three officers were working in COP (or 17.40 percent), it was reasonable to assume that 17.40 percent of utility bills and office supplies should go to COP. Since there is no clear evidence that COP officers spent differently from non-COP officers, all parties finally agreed with Al on the use of this cost base. The operating cost was estimated as $27,731, shown in Table 3.1.

Step 3: Determination of Capital Costs

COP has two capital items—a police patrol vehicle and Electronic Communication Networking (ECN) equipment. The vehicle was purchased and equipped two years ago for $55,000. The car has 26,730 miles on it; the annual average is 13,365 for the first two years. After several calls and an Internet search, Al found that the average lifetime of police vehicles in the city was five years, and the residual market value for a five-year-old car of this type was $4,940. Using the usage rate depreciation method, Al made the following estimation: Vehicle cost of last year = ($55,000 − $4,940)/66,825 × 13,365 = $10,012. Notice that Al assumes that annual mileage on the vehicle is the same for the remaining three years, so total mileages are 66,825 (13,365 × 5). Also, the maintenance for the vehicle is included in office/other supplies.

The ECN is a communication networking system that is shared by all sworn officers in vehicle patrol and bike patrol. The system was purchased five years ago for $1,750,000. The estimated life of the system is ten years, with annual maintenance of $12,470 in the factory contract. The total cost in the lifetime of the system is $1,874,700 ($1,750,000 + ($12,470 × 10)). The system has no residual value.

Al used the "number of patrol hours" as the cost base in the cost allocation. After examining the department patrol records, he found that the annual average of patrol hours was 21,900. So the estimated number of patrol hours for a ten-year period is 219,000. He also knew that COP had 896 patrol hours

Table 3.1

Cost Estimation for the Northenville COP Program

	Salary/ benefit ($) (1)	Total work hours (2)	Hourly rate ($) (3) = (1)/(2)	Hours for COP (4)	Individual personnel cost ($) (3) × (4)
1. Personnel Cost					
Employee					
A	100,852	2,045	49.32	2,045	100,852
B	58,900	2,180	27.02	2,180	58,900
C	68,450	2,080	32.91	832	27,380
D	40,000	2,080	19.23	210	4,039
Total Personnel Cost					191,171
2. Operating Cost ($)					
Uniform and bikes	12,523				
Crime meetings	5,342				
Survey	5,000				
Utility	934				
Office supplies	3,932				
Total operating cost	27,731				
3. Capital Cost ($)					
Police vehicle	10,012				
ENC	7,670				
Total capital cost	17,682				

last year. Using the usage rate depreciation method, he arrived at: ECN cost shared by COP last year = ($1,874,700/219,000) × 896 = $7,670.

Step 4: Determination of Total Program Cost

Table 3.1 shows the result of cost estimation for different cost items. The total program cost was $191,171 + $27,731 + $17,682 = $236,584. Al reported this figure to the city manager. He told the city manager that, according to his previous experiences, there was a +/– 5 percent error margin in this type of estimation. So the true cost was between $224,754 and $248,412.

Neither James nor Edward was happy about this estimation. James argued that Al overestimated some expense items. For example, James said the survey was used for the entire department, not just for the COP program. The cost should not have been counted solely toward the COP program. Edward argued to the contrary. He said Al underestimated the sharing of the ECN cost for the COP. Edward challenged Al's use of "patrol hours" as the cost base. He said Al should have used "patrol miles." He believed COP's patrol miles per officer was far more than that of a non-COP officer.

Step 5: Determination of Average Cost

Nevertheless, the city manager was satisfied with Al's work. She thought that the program was at least at breakeven last year. To strengthen her case to support this program in the upcoming year, she now asked Al to compare the cost of COP with similar programs in other cities.

Al knew that it did not make sense to compare total costs of COP programs as these programs vary greatly in size and activities. He needed to compare the average cost. To calculate the average cost of the COP program, Al needed to first determine the quantity of product for the program. What is a product of the program? Patrols? But patrolling is not the only program activity. The program also organizes crime watch meetings and conducts citizen surveys. After several days of research, Al finally decided to use population as cost base in computing total cost. On average, the COP program spent $5.7 ($236,583/41,200) for each individual citizen.

Exercises

1. Review Key Terms

Public service agencies
Break-even production
Cost
Expenditure
Cost objective
Cost time frame
Cost items (or cost elements)
Total cost (or full cost) (TC)
Average cost (or unit cost) (AC)
Direct cost
Indirect cost
Cost allocation
Overhead rate
Cost base
Cost pool
Activity-based costing (ABC)
Personnel cost
Operating cost
Capital cost
Cost depreciation
Straight-line depreciation

Usage rate depreciation
Average cost as a measure of efficiency

2. Calculations

1. A public administration department at a state university has a master of public administration (MPA) program and a bachelor of public administration (BPA) program. The MPA program has 175 students and the BPA has 134 students. The department has a total indirect cost of $53,340 this year that includes office expenses, utility bills, travel expenses, and other expenses. What is the indirect cost that should be allocated to the MPA program this year if the number of students is the cost base?

2. A city manager of a major urban city makes $124,200 in salary and benefits this year. This amount needs to be allocated to twenty-four programs in the city's program budget that includes an economic development program that promotes employment opportunities and economic growth of the city. It is estimated that the city manager works a total of 1,920 hours a year and about 200 of them are associated with the economic development department. How much of the city manager's salary and benefits should be allocated to the economic development program this year if the number of work hours is the cost base?

3. If the purchase price of a computer network is $12,000 and the computer will be used for three years with a residual value of $2,000 at the end of the three years, what is the annual cost of the network during this period if a straight-line depreciation method is used?

4. In the above question, suppose that the use of the network follows a pattern in which the number of hours in use is 2,920 for Year 1, 2,190 for Year 2, and 1,460 for Year 3. All other conditions are the same. What is the first year's cost of the network if a usage rate deprecation method is used?

3. Determining Cost Base

Cost allocation is one of most difficult tasks in total cost estimation. The use of cost base in cost allocation determines the accuracy of calculation. Two types of measures are often used as cost base. Measures of resource consumption include measures of time spent (e.g., "the number of hours") or manpower used (e.g., "FTE"). Such measures are readily available, so they are inexpensive to use. However, it should be understood that the cost is always associated with an activity of providing a product or service. Scholars sometimes call an activity measure "output measure." Following is a list of "output" cost bases for distribution of administrative or office expenses.

> Accounting cost—the number of invoices processed
> Purchasing cost—the number of purchase orders processed
> Printer cost—the number of reports produced
> Utility—square feet of space assigned
> Telephone—the number of calls made
> Vehicle—the number of miles used

Identify three administrative or office cost items in a governmental agency. Develop two possible cost bases for each cost item.

4. Cost of Operations

U.S. state and local governments are required to report expenses of service functions in a Comprehensive Annual Financial Report (CAFR). Gain access to a recent CAFR. Go to the "Financial Section" of the CAFR and look for the section of "Basic Financial Statements." Turn to "Statement of Activities." Look for the expenses of programs or functions (often listed as the first column). As this statement is prepared on the accrual accounting basis, these annualized expenses can be used to represent the annual cost of these functions or programs. Work in an Excel file to

1. List the three most expensive functions/program activities of the "primary government."
2. Calculate the percentages of each of these function costs in "total primary government."
3. Compare the expenses of these functions over last year's figures to see the difference (last year's figures should be available in last year's CAFR).
4. Write a statement to describe these expense differences.
5. Find the population statistics in the "Statistical Section" of the CAFR. The CAFR should have the population of last ten years. If it doesn't, you need to call the agency to get the figure. Use it to compute "total primary government expenses per capita." Compare it with the number in the previous year to see the trend. Are the services becoming more expensive in this government? Extend this analysis to include the data of the previous three years. Do you observe any trend of cost change in "total primary government expenses per capita" for the past three years?

CHAPTER 4

Cost Comparison

Learning Objectives

After studying this chapter, you should be able to

- Understand the concepts of present value, future value, time value of money, discount rate
- Apply present value of cost in cost comparison
- Apply annualized cost in cost comparison

Suppose you need a computer that costs $1,000. You can pay $1,000 cash right now, or a $500 down payment and $600 next year. If you can afford either option, which one do you take? In this chapter, we learn how to use cost to compare efficiency of programs or decisions. We learn to use present value of cost (PVC) and annualized cost in decision making.

Concepts and the Tool

In the above example, the total payment of the cash option is $1,000, and total payment of the down payment option is $500 + $600 = $1,100. It looks like that the cash option is cheaper. However, it does not make sense to compare these two figures, as the $600 in the down payment option is the payment next year. In finance, this $600 is called the *future value* (FV). The future value is the amount of value realized sometime in the future. To compare these two options, we must place the values of their payments on an equal footing, which requires us to convert the future value into the value of the present day—the *present value* (PV). So the cost comparison question becomes: how to convert the future value to the present value.

How much is this $600 of the next year worth now? We know it is worth less than $600. If we were offered $600 now or in the next year, everyone would take the money now. Economists rationalize this idea that time plays a role in valuation as the *time value of money* (TVM). More specifically, TVM

55

tells us that a given amount of payment (or value) becomes less in the future.

Exactly how much less? To convert a future value to a present value, the following equation can be used.

$$PV = \frac{FV}{(1+i)^N}$$

In the equation, i is called the *discount rate*. It is used to discount the future value. Many people would like to think of it as the interest rate for an investment. The idea is that, if the money isn't spent on the computer, it can be invested and earn interest. So the interest rate determines the discount rate. We can use the interest rate of short-term federal debts (e.g., treasury bills) as a benchmark to determine the discount rate. N in the equation represents the *Nth* project term in the future (a project term is designated as a year in this book).

In the above example, suppose that the discount rate is 5 percent, and N is 1 (one year from now), the PV of $600 in the next year with a 5 percent discount rate is now worth $600/(1 + 0.05)^1 = \$571.43$. So the PV of the down payment option is $500 + $571.43 = $1,071.43, which is $71.43 more than the PV of the cash option. This example illustrates the use of the *present value of cost* (PVC) to make decisions. The PVC can also be calculated from the following equation.

$$PVC = C_0 + \frac{C_1}{(1+i)^1} + \frac{C_2}{(1+i)^2} + \frac{C_3}{(1+i)^3} + \ldots \frac{C_n}{(1+i)^n}$$

In the equation, C_0 is cost in this current term, $C_1, C_2, C_3 \ldots C_n$ are costs in project terms 1, 2, 3 . . . n, and i is the discount rate of the term. In our computer purchase example, the PVC of the down payment option is $C_0 + (C_1)/(1 + i)^1 = \$500 + \$600/(1 + 0.05) = \$500 + \$571.43 = \$1,071.43$.

What is the PVC for a project that costs $500 this year and $600 each year for the next two years? It is $C_0 + (C_1)/(1 + i)^1 + (C_2)/(1 + i)^2 = \$500 + \$600/(1 + 0.05) + \$600/(1 + 0.05)^2 = \$500 + \$571.43 + \$544.22 = \$1,615.65$. We can also use Excel to compute the PV using the following steps.

Step 1: Click "fx" (Paste Function) in the toolbar.
Step 2: Select "Financial" in the Function Category window.
Step 3: Select "NPV" (net present value) in Function Name window.
Step 4: In the NPV window, type interest (or discount) rate, and values.

In our example, we enter 0.05 for "Rate," and $600 each for the "Value 1" and "Value 2" boxes. The present value of $1,115.65 is in the "Formula Result," shown in Excel Screen 4.1. We then need to add $500, the PV of the current term, to arrive at $1,615.65.

Excel Screen 4.1 **Calculating Present Value**

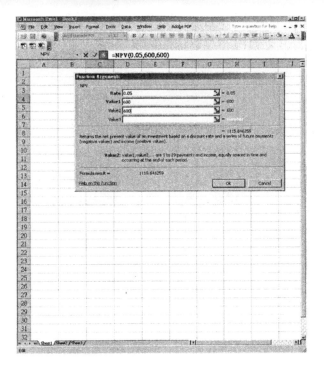

Now, let us change our example a little. Let us say that we have the choice of purchasing Computer A or Computer B. Computer A costs $1,000 cash now and it can be used for three years. Computer B requires a down payment of $500 and a future payment of $600 next year. It can be used for four years. Assume that both computers meet our needs. Which one do we buy?

We know the PVC for Computer A is $1,000 and for Computer B is $1,071.43. Computer A costs less, but lasts one year less. To compare these two options, we need to know the *annualized cost* of each option. The annualized cost of Computer A can be computed from the following equation.

$$\$1,000 = \frac{C}{(1+i)^1} + \frac{C}{(1+i)^2} + \frac{C}{(1+i)^3}$$

C represents annualized cost. Assuming a 5 percent discount rate, the annualized cost is $367.21. This is to say that paying $1,000 now is equivalent to paying $367.21 annually over the next three years. The annualized cost for Computer B is $302.16, a result of solving for C using the equation with a 5 percent discount rate: $\$1,071.43 = C/(1+i)^1 + C/(1+i)^2 + C/(1+i)^3 + C/(1+i)^4$.

Excel Screen 4.2   **Calculating Annualized Cost**

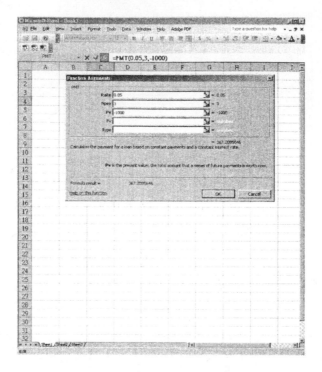

So, for Computer B, paying $1,071.43 now is equal to paying $302.16 every year over the next four years. The result of the annualized cost comparison shows that Computer B costs less than Computer A. The following steps show how to use Excel to calculate annualized cost.

Step 1: Click "fx" (Paste Function) in the toolbar.
Step 2: Select "Financial" in the Function Category window.
Step 3: Select "PMT" (Payment) in the Function Name window.
Step 4: Choose Rate (5 percent in this case), and Nper (the number of payments: three for the Computer A option and four for the Computer B option).
Step 5. Type the present value in the PV box. A negative value should be used for PV, as it is treated as a cost that is being offset. The example of Computer A is shown in Excel Screen 4.2.

So far our calculations have been conducted using an annual basis. The previous examples have used annual future value, annual present value, annual discount rate, and annualized cost. In reality, the term of calculation can be biannual, quarterly, monthly, or daily. The discount rate can be annual, biannual, quarterly, monthly, or daily, depending on the number of time periods used in calculation. For example, if we know monthly future values, and want to convert them into present values, we should use a monthly discount rate, which can be calculated from dividing the annual rate by twelve.

A Case Study

The State University of Greenville, California, has a swimming program for all eligible students. It is an educational program that teaches students how to swim safely. The program coincides with school semesters. Every semester, about thirty spots are open for all registered students. The program is managed by the school's athletic department, which is headed by Joan Nelson. The program hires one full-time and two part-time instructors. It uses a swimming pool facility owned by the school. Students in the program meet every Friday.

The swimming pool facility, named Phrog Pool, in memory of John Phrog who made this facility financially possible, is a forty-year-old facility. Because of its age, maintenance costs have been quite high. For the past several years Joan has been trying to keep the budget of Phrog Pool under control. Two days ago she got a call from the company contracted for the maintenance service of the building. She was told that the heating system broke and the estimate for replacement of the system was more than her total supplementary budget. Joan knew immediately it was the moment to make some decisions.

She had long thought about building a new swimming pool in the same location. However, the university was facing budget cuts. She knew she would have to fight an uphill battle for any new building in her department. To get ready for the upcoming budget season, she wanted a cost comparison of the current maintenance option and a new swimming pool option.

Step 1: Estimation of Project Costs

She asked the contract company to provide an estimate of the annual maintenance cost for the next ten years, including the current year. The estimate is shown in Table 4.1.

She also consulted several swimming pool contractors. The cost of constructing a new swimming pool and the maintenance cost thereafter is shown in Table 4.2.

Step 2: Determination of Present Value of Cost (PVC)

Joan understood that, to compare the costs of the two options, she needed to convert them to PV. To determine the discount rate, she assumed that the

Table 4.1

Estimated Cost of the Maintenance Option

Year	Annual maintenance cost ($)
0 (the current year)	48,000
1	48,000
2	48,000
3	48,000
4	48,000
5	55,000
6	55,000
7	55,000
8	55,000
9	55,000

Table 4.2

Estimated Cost of a New Swimming Pool

Year	Cost of construction and maintenance ($)
0 (the current year)	300,000
1	15,000
2	15,000
3	15,000
4	15,000
5	15,000
6	15,000
7	15,000
8	15,000
9	15,000

university could issue bonds for an annual interest rate of 5 percent. Using Excel, she found that the PVC of the maintenance option with a 5 percent discount rate is $414,109. The PVC for a new swimming pool with a 5 percent discount rate is $406,617.

In other words, although the initial cost seemed to be high for a new swimming pool ($300,000), the option was in fact less costly over the next ten years. The university would be better off by $7,491 over this ten-year period. Although the figure is minor for a ten-year period, Joan argued that, with the second option, the school would have a relatively new swimming facility after ten years. With the first option, the school would be left with a very old swimming pool that desperately needed to be replaced at the end.

Step 3: Making Decisions

Most members in the school's budgetary committee were impressed by Joan's finding and showed an intention to approve a budget request for a new swimming pool. However, a member from the university's School of Business challenged Joan's assumption about the interest rate. He said that a 5 percent interest rate is perhaps too low, as the school does not have a strong credit history and the revenue that would be used to repay the bond was coming from very limited resources, such as student activity fees. He argued that a 10 percent interest rate would be a more proper assumption.

With a 10 percent discount rate, the PVC for the maintenance option is $342,557, compared with the PVC of $386,385 for a new facility. All of sudden, the maintenance option seemed more attractive. In her budget request, Joan decided to present PVC results with both 5 percent and 10 percent discount rates to the budgetary committee to make the decision.

Exercises

1. Review Key Terms

Present value
Future value
Time value of money
Discount rate
Present value of cost
Annualized cost

2. Calculations

1. What is the present value of $1,000 one year from now, with an annual discount rate of 5 percent?
2. What is the present value of $1,000 two years from now, with an annual discount rate of 5 percent?
3. What is the present value of a stream of future values that include $200 now, $500 one year from now, $500 two years from now, and $500 three years from now?
4. What is the annualized cost of $12,000 of computer equipment that lasts five years with an annual discount rate of 5 percent?
5. Suppose that you borrow a ten-year $100,000 loan to purchase a house and the annual interest rate is 7 percent, what should be your monthly payment of principal and interest for the next ten years? (Hint: Use annualized costing and treat annual payments as monthly payments.)

Table 4.3

Cost Estimates for EOP and PMS

Year	EOP ($)	PMS ($)
0 (the current year)	1,500,000	750,000
1	100,000	300,000
2	100,000	300,000
3	100,000	300,000
4	100,000	300,000

6. Suppose the length of the loan is twenty years in Question 5 above, what should be your monthly payment of principal and interest for the next twenty years?

3. Present Value Analysis

The Education Association of Metro Orlando (EAMO) is a public service organization that provides after-school services for children. EAMO recently received a federal grant to improve after-school security for children. The grant amounts to $2 million and will be received over five years. It is designated to improve the communication networking system that monitors the traffic in three school districts. After a comprehensive review of all similar systems available on the market, EAMO identifies two systems that meet its specific need. One is EOP (Electronic Operating Patrol) and another is PMS (Pedestrian Monitoring System). The cost of both systems in the next five years, including the current year, is listed in Table 4.3.

1. Assuming a 5 percent annual discount rate, what are the PVCs for EOP and PMS? Which system should EAMO purchase based on your PVC analysis?
2. Assuming a 10 percent annual discount rate, which system should EAMO purchase?
3. Assume that the life of EOP is six years and that of PMS is five years. Which system should EAMO purchase? Why? (Make assumptions if necessary and explain them.)

4. Present Value Analysis: Lease or Buy Decisions

One of the many uses of PVC and annualized cost is for making a so-called "lease or buy" decision. Suppose that the purchase price of a heavy-duty printer is $19,000, with an annual maintenance cost of $200. And suppose the same printer can be leased for an annual cost of $2,000, with an annual maintenance cost of $300. Consider a fifteen–year term for estimation and a 10 percent annual discount rate. Would it be more cost-efficient to lease or buy? (Explain explicitly any assumption you make.)

CHAPTER 5

Incremental Cost Analysis

Learning Objectives

After studying this chapter, you should be able to

- Understand fixed cost, variable cost, marginal cost, and incremental cost
- Apply marginal cost in decision making
- Apply incremental cost in decision making

Let us say that a city of 20,000 residents would like to provide water and sewer service to an adjacent neighborhood of 1,000 residents. The city's water and sewer treatment program has an annual cost of $2.4 million that includes $500,000 in personnel cost, $1.5 million in operating cost, and $400,000 in annual capital depreciation of a water treatment facility. The average annual cost of the service is $2.4 million/20,000 = $120 per customer. How much does the addition of 1,000 customers cost the city? Some may say $120 × 1,000 = $120,000. However, that may be incorrect. By adding 1,000 new customers, do we really expect a proportional increase in personnel cost, operating cost, and capital cost? Do we plan to hire more employees as the result of additional customers? Do we need an additional investment in the treatment facility? Can the current facility accommodate the additional load?

Suppose that no new investment in the treatment facility is needed, and the personnel cost also remains the same. Operating cost will increase proportionally with the number of customers. As operating cost per customer is $1.5 million/20,000 = $75, the annual cost for the additional 1,000 customers is $75 × 1,000 = $75,000, not $120,000.

In this example, the $75,000 is incremental cost. *Incremental cost analysis* examines cost changes of alternative decisions. It tells how much cost we should expect for a specified decision-making option. Incremental cost is different from total cost and average cost in that it does not consider the cost items that have been incurred in the past. These items, such as personnel and capital costs in the example, are not affected by any new decisions. They have occurred, and will not change for any decision. These costs are called *sunk costs*. Managers can also use incremental cost to weigh up the cost associated with a decision against the incremental revenue. In the above example, the city profits if the estimated annual revenue from the additional 1,000 customers is more than $75,000.

Concepts and the Tool

In previous chapters, we introduced total cost and average cost. These cost concepts are calculated for a given level of product or service quantity. They describe resource consumption in a static state. They do not reflect any change of resource consumption in response to the change of production or service level.

Economists use a different set of concepts to assess the cost associated with the change in product or service quantity. Let us again use the above example. Personnel cost and capital cost do not increase when the number of customers increases. They are fixed cost items in this production. *Fixed cost* (FC) remains constant regardless of the variation in production quantity. Operating cost is a *variable cost* (VC) item, which fluctuates with the variation in production quantity. Realize that the *total cost* (TC) is the sum of fixed costs and variable costs (TC = FC + VC).

It is possible that a fixed cost item changes for a larger variation of quantity. For example, when the number of additional water/sewer customers increases by 2,000, the city needs to hire new staff to handle billing. Personnel cost becomes a variable cost at this point. So fixed cost is "fixed" only for a particular *quantity range*. Sometimes it is difficult to classify a cost item as fixed or variable. For example, electricity cost is a fixed cost when the use is for lighting and a variable cost when used for the oven (more cooking, more consumption). These cost items are called *mixed costs.*

Incremental cost (IC) is the change in cost due to a production quantity change or change of decision options. If we use Δ to represent incremental change, then IC can be defined as

$$IC = \Delta TC = \Delta FC + \Delta VC$$

ΔTC is change in total cost. ΔFC is change in fixed cost. ΔVC is change in variable cost. Sometimes it is useful to calculate incremental cost for unit change in quantity. This is the concept of *marginal cost* (MC).

$$MC = \Delta TC / \Delta Q$$

Table 5.1

Incremental Cost Analysis

Quantity (number of students)	FC ($)	VC ($)	TC ($)	AC ($)	IC ($)	MC ($)
1,000	5,000,000	4,000,000	9,000,000	. . .	. . .	. . .
1,200	5,000,000	4,800,000	9,800,000	8,167	800,000	4,000

ΔTC is change in total cost. ΔQ is change in production quantity. In the above water/sewer example, ΔTC is $75,000 and ΔQ is 1,000. So MC = $75,000/1,000 = $75. The interpretation is that the cost for serving each additional water/sewer customer is $75.

Let us look at another example. Suppose that an elementary school has 1,000 students. The fixed cost for running the school includes full-time faculty and staff salaries and benefits, land, and school building and classrooms, which total $5 million a year. The variable cost includes utilities, office expenses, and part-time staff salaries and benefits. The variable cost increases with an increase in the number of students, and each enrolled student incurs $4,000. The total variable cost for the 1,000 students is $1,000 \times \$4,000 = \$4$ million. The total cost, including the $5 million in fixed costs and the $4 million in variable costs, is $9 million.

Let us say the school authority would like to increase student enrollment to 1,200. What is the cost of adding 200 students? How much more should the school propose in the budget to cover the cost of the additional 200 students? The fixed cost does not change—no new buildings and no new hiring of full-time faculty and staff are required. The variable cost increases proportionally with new students. So the addition of 200 students will increase the variable cost to $1,200 \times \$4,000 = \$4.8$ million. The total cost for the 1,200-student enrollment is $9.8 million. The incremental cost is $9.8 million – $9.0 million = $800,000. The marginal cost is $4,000 (($9.8 million – $9.0 million)/(1,200 – 1,000)). Therefore, the school should propose an increase of $800,000 in total budget, equal to an average of $4,000 for each new student. Table 5.1 shows the process of calculation.

Notice that the school should not use the average cost to determine the budget for the new students. Why? The average cost at the 1,200-student level is $8,167. It includes fixed costs that do not increase for adding new students. If the school authority uses the average cost, it will wrongly inflate the cost for adding new students.

Now, suppose the number of new students increases to 1,500 from the 1,200 level two years from now. To accommodate this increase, some fixed cost items

Table 5.2

Incremental Cost Analysis (Continued)

Quantity (number of students)	FC ($)	VC ($)	TC ($)	AC ($)	IC ($)	MC ($)
1,000	5,000,000	4,000,000	9,000,000	9,000	. . .	. . .
1,200	5,000,000	4,800,000	9,800,000	8,167	800,000	4,000
1,500	7,000,000	6,000,000	13,000,000	8,667	3,200,000	10,667

will increase. Suppose that fixed cost increases to $7.0 million. What are the incremental and marginal costs? Since the variable cost increases to $4,000 × 1,500 = $6.0 million, the total cost is $13.0 million. The incremental cost for the additional 300 students is $13.0 million – $9.8 million = $3.2 million. The marginal cost is $3.2 million/300 = $10,667. Table 5.2 shows the calculations.

A Case Study

One application of incremental cost analysis is in outsourcing or contracting-out decisions. Spring Park Health Foundation (SPHF) of North Carolina is a public service organization that provides child health care and family services in the metropolitan area of Spring Park, an area of 650,000 residents. SPHF has undertaken three major projects. A school nurse program provides school-age children with immediate access to nurses and medication. A comprehensive health care program offers a wide range of counseling services to school children and their families. SPHF also operates an education program that trains school teachers about health care issues. For example, one recent training workshop disseminated the latest research results on nutrition.

The foundation had a budget of $7.5 million last year. Eighty percent of the budget, about $6.0 million, came from the investment income of a trust fund. A state grant provided $1.3 million (17.3 percent of the total budget). The remaining 2.7 percent, about $200,000, came from miscellaneous sources, such as office rental, sale of publications, and a very insignificant charge on heavy users of school nurses. The state grant is audited and approved on an annual basis, subject to the results of an annual performance audit on the foundation's programs. To satisfy the need for the audit, the foundation has an evaluation team that consists of three full-time evaluators. Every year, the team produces a performance audit of the whole foundation and a program evaluation for each of the three programs. The annual budget of the evaluation is $345,000, which includes $220,000 in personnel services, $50,000 in office rental, $12,000 in office equipment, $10,000 in transportation, $13,000 in office supplies, and $40,000 in printing and binding.

As a result of declining investment returns in a downward stock market, the foundation faced a tougher budget this year. One proposal to deal with the budget decline was to cut back the evaluation team and contract out the evaluation to a private firm. Nancy Winston, the foundation program coordinator, was responsible for soliciting bids. Of the three firms that participated in the bidding, one asked for a fee of $450,000 and was immediately rejected. The second firm asked a fee of $330,000. The third bidder, a state university, asked $310,000. Both bidders guaranteed the quality of the reports. Should Nancy accept the lower bid?

Step 1: Examining Each Cost Item

The purpose of this step is to determine the cost change as the result of contracting out. During this step, Nancy found that the following costs would be eliminated if the evaluation team were contracted out: personnel services, transportation, office supplies, and printing and binding. Since the evaluation team rents office space from the foundation, the cost reduction would be offset by the revenue loss of the same amount to the foundation. So this cost would not be eliminated if the evaluation was contracted out. Also, the evaluation team owns two computers and uses a network printer. The cost associated with this equipment would not be immediately saved through contracting out.

Step 2: Determining Incremental Cost (or Marginal Cost, If Necessary)

Table 5.3 shows the cost comparison of the current in-house operation and the lower bid contracting-out option. The incremental cost of the contracting-out option is the change in total cost due to the contracting out. The result in the table shows a $27,000 increase if the foundation contracts out.

Step 3: Making Decisions

Based on the analysis, Nancy decided to reject the proposal of contracting out. She, however, showed a willingness to reconsider if the university reduced its consulting fee to a figure that was significantly less than $283,000.

Exercises

1. Key Terms

Sunk cost
Fixed cost (FC)
Variable cost (VC)
Quantity range

Table 5.3

Cost Comparison in Incremental Cost Analysis

	TC for in-house evaluation team ($) (1)	TC of contracting out ($) (2)	Incremental cost ($) (2) − (1)
Personnel services	220,000	0	−220,000
Office rental	50,000	50,000	0
Office equipment	12,000	12,000	0
Transportation	10,000	0	−10,000
Office supplies	13,000	0	−13,000
Printing and binding	40,000	0	−40,000
Consulting fee	0	310,000	310,000
Total	345,000	372,000	27,000

Mixed cost
Incremental cost (IC)
Marginal cost (MC)

2. Calculations

Table 5.4 shows the cost information for a product at the 15,000-units level.

1. What are the incremental and marginal costs for producing 5,000 additional units?
2. Suppose that, at a new production level of 30,000, the fixed cost increases to $4.5 million, what are the incremental and marginal costs for the additional 10,000 units?

3. Incremental Cost Analysis

A county's recycling program collected 46,280 tons of recyclable refuse this year. The cost of the program includes five vehicles that can partly process the recycles. The county does not have depreciation information for these trucks. But they estimate annual maintenance costs of up to $10,000 for each truck. The fuel expense totaled $69,000 this year. The county also hires fifty workers in the program. The annual personnel expense this year was $1.5 million. Other expenses this year included office expenses of $15,000, overhead of $189,000, and miscellaneous expenses of $150,000.

Recently, a small nearby city asked the county to provide recycling services. The city offered a fixed fee of $6.00 for every ton of recyclable material pickup. It is estimated that there will be 3,500 tons of pickup during

Table 5.4

Incremental Costing Exercise

Quantity	FC ($)	VC ($)	TC ($)	IC ($)	MC ($)
15,000	3,000,000	1,500,000	?	. . .	. . .
20,000	?	?	?	?	?
30,000	?	?	?	?	?

the next year from the city.

County analysts studied the proposal. They reckoned that, to add 3,500 tons of pickup, the county did not need new vehicles or new hiring. Office and miscellaneous expenses would also remain the same. But, the fuel consumption and the overhead would increase.

Treating fuel and overhead as variable costs and others as fixed costs, calculate the incremental cost and marginal cost for the county. Should the county accept the city's offer? Discuss in detail the logic of your decision. Explain explicitly any assumption you make.

4. Incremental Cost Analysis

Referring to the above problem, suppose that the city wants a two-year deal. In the second year of the deal, the recycling materials from the city will be 5,000 tons. The county analysis shows that a new vehicle is needed for the increase. The estimated purchasing price of the vehicle is $30,000, and the annual maintenance cost is the same, $10,000.

Considering this change, and also treating the fuel and the overhead as variable costs and others as fixed costs, calculate the incremental cost and marginal cost for the county. If the city still wants to pay the same rate for the service, $6.00 a ton, should the county accept the offer? (Note: Use annual maintenance cost for the vehicle in the calculation.)

5. Incremental Cost Analysis and Zero-Based Budgeting

Incremental cost analysis is a potentially useful tool for zero-based budgeting (ZBB). ZBB requires the development of program costs in an agency's budget request. The programs need to be evaluated and ranked according to their relative importance to the agency's mission. Decision makers then make funding decisions based on the relative importance of a program and its cost. Conduct an Internet search on the topic of ZBB to identify an agency, if any, that claims to use ZBB. Study its ZBB budget to find out whether IC is used, and if not, discuss how to use it to enhance the budget.

CHAPTER 6

Cost-Benefit Analysis

Learning Objectives

After studying this chapter, you should be able to

- Calculate the net present value and the benefit/cost ratio
- Understand conditions to which a cost-benefit analysis applies
- Apply the cost-benefit analysis in decision making

If you buy a house that costs $10,000 a year, and you earn revenue of $15,000 by renting it out, your annual profit is $5,000. You have made a good financial decision. In economics, a decision that can bring profit is described as "economically feasible."

Concepts and the Tool

Introduction to Cost-Benefit Analysis

Cost-benefit analysis (CBA) assesses the economic feasibility of a program, policy, or activity. It rationalizes decision making through careful examination of a program's objectives and the costs and benefits associated with the program. It is useful when decision makers are required to judge the economic value of a program or choose one program among several options. For this reason, CBA can be used to evaluate capital projects in budgeting. This chapter focuses on the use of CBA in capital budgeting.

The first step in CBA is to predict costs and benefits of a project. As capital projects often take multiple years, the forecast involves the estimation of multiple-year costs and benefits in the future. For the purpose of comparison, the future value of costs and benefits must be converted to the present value (review Chapter 4, "Cost Comparison," for the discussion of present value and future value). The result of the comparison is *net present value* (NPV).

NPV = Present Value of Benefits (or PVB) –
Present Value of Costs (or PVC)

Let us look at a five-year project that costs $1,000 in the first year (the current year) and $200 every year from the second to the fifth year. Let us assume a 5 percent discount rate. The PVC for the project is $1,000 + ($200)/$(1.05)^1$ + ($200)/$(1.05)^2$ + ($200)/$(1.05)^3$ + ($200)/$(1.05)^4$ = $1,709 (review Chapter 4 for the PVC calculation). Suppose that the project has an annual revenue of $500 beginning with the first year (the current year), for five years. Its PVB is $500 + ($500)/$(1.05)^1$ + ($500)/$(1.05)^2$ + ($500)/$(1.05)^3$ + ($500)/$(1.05)^4$ = $2,273. Therefore, the NPV = $564 ($2,273 – $1,709). Similar to the way PVC is defined in Chapter 4, PVB is defined here as

$$PVB = B_0 + \frac{B_1}{(1+i)^1} + \frac{B_2}{(1+i)^2} + \frac{B_3}{(1+i)^3} + \ldots \frac{B_n}{(1+i)^n}$$

<B_0, B_1, B_2, B_3 . . . B_n are benefits generated by the project in project terms 0, 1, 2, 3 . . . n (B_0 is the current term's benefit), and i is the discount rate of the project term (the project term is designated in years in this book).

In CBA, a project is economically feasible when its NPV is positive (NPV > 0), which means that project benefits exceed project costs. If there are two projects and only one can be funded, and both projects will produce a positive NPV, then the one that has a larger positive NPV should be chosen.

In addition to NPV, the *benefit/cost ratio,* defined as PVB/PVC, can also be used to make the decision. Since NPV = PVB – PVC, when NPV > 0, (PVB – PVC) > 0, or PVB > PVC, or PVB/PVC > 1. This means that, when the NPV is larger than zero, the benefit/cost ratio is larger than 1. The benefit/cost ratio represents the benefit received for every dollar of cost. For example, a ratio of 0.5 means a half dollar benefit is earned for every dollar of cost. Of course, both benefits and costs are in the form of the present value.

Even if a project is economically feasible, that doesn't necessarily mean that it will be funded. Students of American public administration should know that funding decisions are the result of a political process in which economic value is only part of the consideration.

Let us look at a simplified CBA example. A city faces an increasing demand for its garbage collection service. Two options have been considered to improve the city's garbage collection capacity. Option A requires the purchase of a garbage collection vehicle that needs a three-person crew. The vehicle will cost $50,000 and each worker will be paid $20,000 a year. The city would pick up 400 tons of garbage annually, and for each ton of garbage collected, it would charge a $400 fee. The city would have annual revenue of $160,000 (400 × $400) from this operation.

Table 6.1

CBA for Garbage Pickup Options ($)

Year	Present value of cost	Present value of benefit
Option A		
0 (the current year)	$50,000 + 60,000 = 110,000$	$400 \times \$400 = 160,000$
1	$60,000/(1 + 5\%) = 57,143$	$160,000/(1 + 5\%) = 152,381$
2	$60,000/(1 + 5\%)^2 = 54,422$	$160,000/(1 + 5\%)^2 = 145,125$
3	$60,000/(1 + 5\%)^3 = 51,830$	$160,000/(1 + 5\%)^3 = 138,214$
4	$60,000/(1 + 5\%)^4 = 49,362$	$160,000/(1 + 5\%)^4 = 131,632$
Total	322,757	727,352

NPV for Option A is $727,352 - 322,757 = 404,595$

Year	Present value of cost	Present value of benefit
Option B		
0 (the current year)	$90,000 + 40,000 = 130,000$	$300 \times \$400 = 120,000$
1	$40,000/(1 + 5\%) = 38,095$	$120,000/(1 + 5\%) = 114,286$
2	$40,000/(1 + 5\%)^2 = 36,281$	$120,000/(1 + 5\%)^2 = 108,843$
3	$40,000/(1 + 5\%)^3 = 34,554$	$120,000/(1 + 5\%)^3 = 103,661$
4	$40,000/(1 + 5\%)^4 = 32,908$	$120,000/(1 + 5\%)^4 = 98,724$
Total	271,838	545,514

NPV for Option B is $545,514 - 271,838 = 273,676$

Option B requires a vehicle for a two-person crew. The vehicle will cost $90,000 and each worker will be paid $20,000 annually. With this option, the city's garbage collection capacity would be 300 tons annually, so the annual revenue would be $120,000 ($300 \times $400). Using a five-year period and a discount rate of 5 percent, which option should be recommended in the budget request? Table 6.1 shows the CBA analysis for these two options.

Since the NPV of Option A is larger than that of Option B, Option A should be recommended in the capital budget request.

Issues in Cost-Benefit Analysis

Although CBA is a useful tool, it is not applicable for every project. When it is applied, it is important to ensure it is done right. In this section, we discuss some critical issues concerning how to do CBA.

Measuring Benefits

First, a clearly defined and achievable project objective is needed. For example, a highway project that connects two busy districts in a metropolitan area can be designed to reduce traffic accidents and save travelers' time. Time saving is a clearly defined and achievable objective of the project. The "achievable" means that designated project results can be empirically observed.

Many projects have multiple project objectives. For example, in addition to time saving, a goal of the highway project is also reducing traffic accidents. Both time saving and accident reduction are project objectives. For multiple objectives, we need to determine whether they are *mutually inclusive*—the fulfillment of one affects another. For example, if we determine that a highway with reduced accidents also saves travelers' time, then time saving and accident reduction are two mutually inclusive objectives. Mutual inclusion of objectives indicates that benefits of two objectives are also mutually inclusive, and that caution should be exercised to avoid double-counting of benefits. On the other hand, if a project has two *mutually exclusive* benefits, both should be included in the analysis. For example, an educational program benefits both employees and business owners. The benefit to employees is mutually exclusive from that to owners.

Second, an objective should be measurable and quantifiable. Time saving can be measured by "the amount of time saved for an average traveler daily." Accident reduction can be measured by "the number of accidents daily." There are different types of measures, such as *outputs* and *outcomes,* that can be used to measure project benefits. Outputs are a project's direct products or immediate results. An example of an output for a job-training program is "the number of people trained" or "the number of training hours produced." Outcomes refer to a project's intermediate or long-term impact and achievement. An outcome of the job-training program is an increase in the employment rate or, more specifically, "the percentage of trainees who are employed again" after a period of time. In general, the relationship between a project and its outcomes is difficult to observe empirically; therefore outcomes may be less useful than outputs in determining project benefits. For instance, can we really credit the training program for the improvement of the employment rate? Or could the economy and characteristics of the job market also play a role? Oftentimes, it is difficult to distinguish project impact from other nonproject factors on an outcome.

Third, project benefits must be converted to monetary gain. The benefit of a garbage collection project can be converted to gains in revenue. A traveler's time saving can be transformed into his or her financial gain. This monetary conversion is critical to CBA. When it is impossible or very costly to measure benefits in monetary terms, we may apply *cost-effectiveness analysis* (CEA).

Suppose that we compare two possible highway projects designed to reduce the number of traffic accidents. Project A costs $10 million in present value during a ten-year period, and Project B costs $14 million. The benefit of the projects is "the number of traffic accidents reduced." Suppose that Project A can reduce the accidents by 1,000 counts and Project B by 1,500 counts, then the present value of cost for each accident reduced is $10,000,000/1,000 = $10,000 for Project A and $14,000,000/1,500 = $9,333 for Project B. We will choose Project B because it is more cost-effective. In CEA, we compute a project's present value of cost for its designated effectiveness. There is another example of CEA in the exercises below, but a full discussion of this technique is beyond the scope of this book.

Finally, measuring benefits becomes controversial when social values are considered or human lives are involved. Which project do you prefer—one that saves one life a year and costs $1 million, or the second one that saves two lives but costs $10 million? What is the value of human lives? What is the value of your own life? Another difficult issue in CBA is to determine benefits and costs to "whom." A project laying off workers to reduce costs may be beneficial to an organization, but costly to society.

Estimating Costs

There is a difference between the *project cost* (accounting cost) and the *opportunity cost*. The former is the summation of all the resources consumed by the project during its lifetime. It includes all cost items associated with producing a product or a service. The estimation of these cost items is discussed in Chapter 3. What is opportunity cost? Think about the cost of getting a graduate degree. Is it tuition? Many would perhaps disagree. Many value family time greatly, and if it is lost because of time spent on an education, then the opportunity cost of the education can be the value of family time lost. In general, the opportunity cost of a project is the value of the best alternative forgone because of the project. If the project cost is the resource consumed for Project A, the opportunity cost of Project A is the value of the best alternative project forgone because of Project A.

Choosing the Discount Rate

Discounting is necessary when benefits or costs stretch over several years in the future. Both benefits and costs must be converted to present value for comparison. The discount rate, or the *opportunity rate of return,* adjusts costs and benefits to their present values. In theory, the discount rate of a project is determined by the answer to the question: What is the return of the best alternative to the current project? If, instead of investing in the current project, the best investment option of the money will bring a 5 percent increase in value in a short-term government bond fund, then the discount rate is 5 percent. If the best alternative investment option is a high-yield cooperate bond that would bring 10 percent interest, the discount rate is 10 percent.

A Case Study

The Public Works Department in Sunny Village, California, has a mechanical shop responsible for maintaining the city's vehicles. The shop director, Steven Douglas, has five employees and a budget of $845,000 this year. In addition to regular check-up and maintenance services, the shop also provides short classes to city employees on how to efficiently operate cars and trucks. The goal of the shop is to let no vehicles break down in service. But breakdowns do happen. When they happen, a diagnostic check-up is performed to find out the possible cause.

The current diagnostic system was purchased five years ago. It is a manual tester, called Vehicle Testing Monitor 2000 (or VTM 2000). It includes a communicator that connects a vehicle with a computer screen. A vehicle consists of several major systems (engine, electric circuit system, fuel system, and steering system, etc.). Each system also has accessory parts. If one part breaks, the whole system fails to work. To find out the problem part, a mechanic needs to connect the VTM with the vehicle system. If a system consists of several parts, VTM has to check these parts one by one until the problem part is identified. Figure 6.1 shows a diagnostic process for a system that has three accessory parts.

Steven believes the VTM is slow in diagnosis, and yields a high possibility of replacing good parts. In this year's budget request, Steven requested a new diagnostic system, Quality Test System (or QTS). QTS includes an information database, test instrument module, and expert diagnostic software system. During a diagnosis, a mechanic first enters a vehicle's identification code. After analyzing the meter readouts and problem symptoms, the expert system identifies the problem part and then gives repair instructions, shown on a computer monitor. So, instead of a step-by-step diagnosis for each part at a time by VTM, QTS checks all parts of a system simultaneously. Figure 6.2 shows how it works for a system that has three parts.

In a recent budget preparation meeting, Steven presented his case to his supervisor, Public Works Director Lisa Jones. He estimated that the price of QTS was $21,400. The estimated operating cost was $280 each year. The estimated life of the system was six years (including the current year).

He estimated that the benefits of QTS would come from two sources.

Figure 6.1 **VTM Diagnostic Process**

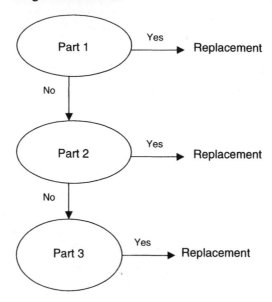

First, diagnosis would be quicker, so diagnostic time would be saved. Diagnostic time is the time from the beginning of a diagnosis to the discovery of problem. The VTM's multiple-step diagnostic process would be replaced by a single-step process of QTS. Time saving for each diagnosis problem would differ. For instance, it takes VTM 45 to 60 minutes to test an infected flow, compared to 3 minutes by QTS. For most engine problems, VTM needs 60 to 120 minutes, compared to 10 minutes by QTS. Steven estimated that, on average for each diagnosis, VTM would take150 minutes, while QTS would take about 30.

The city has ninety vehicles: thirty police cars and sixty trucks. All the vehicles are in relatively good shape. The police cars are replaced every two years. Only a small number of vehicles need diagnosis. The mechanic shop in the department does fifty-two diagnoses a year (once a week for fifty-two weeks a year). Also, on average, a mechanic's hourly wage and benefits are $12.

The second major benefit comes from accurate diagnosis. QTS is more accurate than VTM in diagnosis. With VTM, mechanics are more likely to mistakenly replace a good part. This is called ineffective replacement. With the new system, the problem part could be identified accurately. Cost for ineffective replacement is $50 a diagnosis for VTM. This cost for QTS would be $0. Finally, Steven said, "if we get QTS, we can sell VTM for about $692 in today's market." Lisa thought Steven's analysis was too broad and asked for a CBA.

Figure 6.2 **QTS Diagnosis**

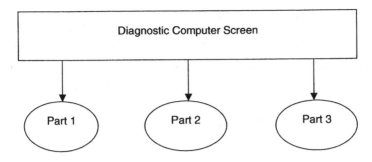

Step 1: Formulating the Question in Cost-Benefit Analysis

First, there is no need to conduct CBA for the existing system VTM. The decision of purchasing the system was made and the cost associated with VTM is a sunk cost. To estimate the cost and benefit of QTS, we need to know the objective of the vehicle diagnostic system. The goal of the mechanic shop of the Public Works Department is stated as "protection of the city's vehicles through efficient and effective maintenance and repair." So the CBA question can be formulated as: What are the costs and benefits of purchasing QTS in maintaining and repairing the city's vehicles?

Step 2: Determining the Benefit

First, we need to identify the benefits that should be included in CBA. Three QTS benefits serve the goal of the mechanic shop—diagnostic time saving, improved diagnostic accuracy, and residual value of the old system if it is sold. Second, benefits should be converted to monetary terms. For diagnostic time saving, salary and benefits information are needed. As we know, QTS saves two hours (150 minutes – 30 minutes) for each diagnosis and, for fifty-two diagnoses a year, there would be a saving of $1,248 a year (two hours × fifty-two weeks × $12 per hour). We also know that QTS is more accurate in diagnosis. By reducing ineffective replacement of parts, the system would save $50 on each diagnosis, for an annual saving of $2,600 ($50 × 52). The last benefit is the salvage value of selling the VTM. The market value is estimated at $692. Table 6.2 presents the PVB calculation for QTS (refer to Chapter 4 for using Excel in the process of converting the future value to the present value).

Table 6.2

Present Value of Benefits for QTS ($)

Year	Time saving	Accurate diagnosis	Salvage value
0 (the current year)	1,248	2,600	692
1	1,135	2,364	0
2	1,031	2,149	0
3	938	1,953	0
4	852	1,776	0
5	775	1,614	0
Total	5,979	12,456	692

Note: Discount rate = 10 percent.

Table 6.3

Present Value of Costs for QTS ($)

Year	Purchasing cost	Operating cost
0 (the current year)	21,400	280
1	0	254
2	0	231
3	0	210
4	0	191
5	0	174
Total	21,400	1,340

Note: Discount rate = 10 percent.

Step 3: Determining the Cost

The purchase cost of QTS is $21,400 with an annual operating cost of $280. Table 6.3 shows the process of calculating PVC.

Step 4: Determining the Discount Rate

Lisa believes that if the project is approved, the funding will come from a capital project fund that is funded by city debts. The city now pays an approximate 10 percent interest rate for issuing long-term debts. So the discount rate is appropriate at 10 percent.

Step 5: Calculating the Net Present Value

The PVB of QTS is $19,127 ($5,979 + $12,456 + $692). The PVC is $22,741 ($21,400 + $1,340). Thus, NPV = PVB – PVC = $19,127 – $22,741 = –$3,614. For the lifetime of six years, a CBA on QTS shows a NPV of –$3,614.

Step 6: Making Decisions

Since NPV is negative, the funding of QTS does not appear to be economically feasible. So a decision was made not to fund QTS. Steven argued back. He said that the number of diagnoses was based on this year's data. The number should double to two vehicle diagnoses a week. Would this change the NPV of the QTS and therefore the funding decision?

Exercises

1. Key Terms

Cost-benefit analysis (CBA)
Net present value (NPV)
Present value of benefits
Benefit/cost ratio
Achievable project objectives
Mutually inclusive project objectives
Mutually exclusive project objectives
Measurable and quantifiable project objectives
Project outcomes
Project outputs
Project (accounting) cost
Opportunity cost
Cost-effectiveness analysis (CEA)

2. Calculations

Table 6.4 shows cost and benefit flows of two public infrastructure projects.

1. Use a 5 percent discount rate to compute the NPV for both projects.
2. Recalculate the NPV for both projects with a 10 percent discount rate.
3. Write a paragraph to discuss the economic feasibility of the two projects.

3. The Sensitivity Analysis in CBA

In CBA, assumptions must be made about benefits, costs, the discount rate, and the lifetime of a project. In reality, these assumptions change. For example, in this chapter's Sunny Village case study, the discount rate can be lower if the interest rate of the city's long-term debt is lower. The change of assumption

Table 6.4

Cost-Benefit Analysis for Two Public Infrastructure Projects ($)

Year	Personnel	Operating	Capital	Benefit
		Cost		
Project A				
0 (the current year)	300,000	0	200,000	0
1	150,000	2,000	100,000	0
2	100,000	15,000	25,000	30,000
3	0	21,000	0	150,000
4	0	21,000	0	200,000
5	0	21,000	0	200,000
6	0	21,000	0	200,000
7	0	21,000	0	200,000
8	0	25,000	0	200,000
9	0	25,000	0	200,000
10	0	25,000	0	200,000
Project B				
0 (the current year)	500,000	0	125,000	0
1	100,000	12,500	25,000	187,500
2	0	25,000	0	187,500
3	0	25,000	0	187,500
4	0	25,000	0	187,500
5	0	25,000	0	187,500
6	0	25,000	0	187,500
7	0	25,000	0	187,500
8	0	25,000	0	187,500
9	0	25,000	0	187,500
10	0	25,000	0	187,500

inevitably changes CBA results. The type of analysis that examines the impact of assumption change on CBA results is called sensitivity analysis.

1. Now, assume that the discount rate is reduced from 10 percent to 5 percent, and everything else is unchanged, conduct a CBA for Sunny Village's Diagnostic System.
2. Conduct a CBA in which the cost of ineffective replacement increases to $65, with everything else unchanged.
3. Finally, if the city decides to purchase QTS regardless of the CBA results, but wants to extend its lifetime of use until a positive NPV is produced, how long should the city keep QTS?

4. Cost-Effectiveness Analysis

Sometimes it is rather difficult to convert benefits into monetary gains. In the Sunny Village case, we can choose not to convert the benefit to monetary terms, but rather, measure the benefit by "the number of vehicles diagnosed correctly the first time." With PVC, we can calculate a ratio that indicates PVC for one correct diagnosis. This is a case of cost-effectiveness analysis.

Here is another example of cost-effectiveness analysis. A school district is considering two options for a new school. Option A has a capacity to accommodate 1,000 students in the first year and an annual increase of 100 thereafter. The option costs $10.0 million in the first year and $2.5 million annually thereafter. Option B offers spaces for 300 students in the first year, with an annual increase of 200 students every year thereafter. The plan costs $7.0 million in the first year and $3.0 million annually thereafter. Consider a seven-year term and a 5 percent discount rate. Conduct a cost-effectiveness analysis for the options. Which option should the school choose?

5. CBA for Education

Conduct a CBA for obtaining a master's degree from a public college. Explain explicitly any assumptions in your analysis.

PART II

TOOLS FOR FINANCIAL IMPLEMENTATION

CHAPTER 7

Financial Performance Monitoring

Learning Objectives

After studying this chapter, you should be able to

- Determine proper indicators for monitoring
- Detect unacceptable performance
- Detect performance trends
- Develop a complete picture of financial performance
- Identify causes of underperformance
- Take proper actions to improve performance

Imagine that your family has budgeted $400 per month on entertainment, but when the credit card bill comes, it turns out that $500 has been spent. A budget monitoring system, balancing the credit card bill in this case, tells you that you have overspent, and that you need to limit your subsequent spending to balance the budget.

A financial monitoring system serves three purposes. First, it provides an ongoing check on the budget. By comparing actual financial results against budgets, it can be determined how well financial objectives have been achieved, and whether the budget is realistic. In the above example, if the family keeps spending more than $400 on entertainment, that is an indication that the budget of $400 is too low and should be increased.

Second, a monitoring system helps uncover inefficient practices and operations. In the above case, maybe the family spends too much on popcorn and drinks at the movie because they attend late-afternoon matinees when they are becoming hungry for dinner. Overspending on snacks could be avoided by going to the movies in the evening, just after dinner. Of course, a monitoring system can also discover desirable practices and operations. A consistent revenue surplus uncovered by a monitoring system may indicate enhanced efforts in revenue collection, and such efforts should be encouraged. Nevertheless, detection of inefficient and undesirable behaviors should be the focus of a monitoring system, as the costs of such behaviors, if not corrected quickly, are often high.

Third, and perhaps most important, a monitoring system helps avoid further deterioration of financial condition. Imagine that, in the above case, the overspending goes unnoticed for long enough that you have trouble paying your entertainment bill. The consequences of such behavior are paying unusually high interest or penalties, or in rare cases of personal finance, filing for personal bankruptcy. Severe financial consequences have occurred in the case of governments. Orange County, California, made poor investment choices and filed for bankruptcy in 1994. In 1996, the City of Miami had an enormous budget deficit that sent the city to the brink of financial insolvency.

Concepts and the Tool

Financial performance monitoring is a system designed to detect undesirable financial performance and provide possible solutions to enhance performance. Three essential elements are needed in developing an effective financial monitoring system. They are:

- Indicators that assess financial performance
- Techniques to detect unacceptable financial performance
- Techniques to diagnose causes of underperformance and to provide suggestions for performance improvement

Determining Monitoring Indicators

What Indicators Are Available?

Numerous indicators are used to evaluate a wide range of organizational objectives and operations. These indicators can be broken down into two categories: *financial indicators,* which evaluate an organization's financial operations and financial condition, and *nonfinancial indicators,* which assess elements of an organization's performance that are not characterized by financial transactions, financial operations, or monetary success. Examples of nonfinancial performance indicators include citizen/client satisfaction measures.

Financial indicators can be further classified into three categories: *financial input indicators, financial process indicators,* and *financial results indicators.* Financial input indicators assess the availability of financial resources and the level of financial resource consumption. Indicators 1 and 2, defined below, are in this category.

Indicator 1: Total Revenue or Revenue Per Capita. The variations of *total revenue* include *total revenue by fund* and *revenues by source* (i.e., taxes, fees, charges, intergovernmental revenues), which indicate the level of resources available for service provision. The percentage of a particular revenue in total revenue can also be monitored to assess whether an organization overrelies on the revenue. For example, the *percentage of intergovernmental revenues in total revenue* (Intergovernmental Revenues/Total Revenue) can be used to evaluate how much an organization relies on the revenues from other governments. *Revenue per capita* (Total Revenue/Population) demonstrates the revenue in relation to population, which measures resources available for each individual resident served. This indicator controls the impact of population on resources, and is a better measure of resource availability for a community with a changing population.

Indicator 2: Total Expenditures or Expenditures Per Capita. One variation of *total expenditures* is the *expenditures by function*, such as personnel, operating, or capital expenditures. These indicators assess the level of resources consumed for service provision. The percentage of a particular expenditure in total expenditures can also be monitored to identify major expenditure items. *Expenditures per capita* (Total Expenditure/Population) measures resource consumption for each individual resident.

Financial process indicators are used to address issues in financial operations, such as cash liquidity, borrowing capacity, operating deficits, pension liability, and capital outlays. Monitoring financial process indicators is often tailored to a specific monitoring need. For example, a manager may be concerned about cash liquidity as the result of a recent purchase of an expensive capital item. Or operation deficits become the center of discussion among managers due to a recent economic slowdown and erosion of tax bases. Indicators 3 to 6, described below, are process indicators.

Indicator 3: Liquidity. Liquidity evaluates whether an organization has enough cash and cash equivalents to meet its short-term obligations. Insufficient liquidity affects an organization's financial viability. Excessive liquidity suggests possible loss of investment opportunity. One common liquidity indicator is the *current ratio* (Current Assets/Current Liabilities). *Current assets* are cash, cash equivalents, or assets convertible to cash within one year. Cash equivalents are assets that can be easily converted to cash. They often include marketable securities, money owed by others in exchange for goods and services (accounts receivable), and inventory. *Current liabilities* are obligations that are expected to be paid within one year. They mainly include the amount an organization owes to suppliers for equipment or product purchases and to employees for wages and benefits. In accounting, many of these expenses are reported in payable accounts. A rule of thumb for an acceptable current ratio is 2.0. Any value smaller should cause concern about liquidity. We will further study current assets and current liabilities in Chapter 9.

Indicator 4: Net Assets or Change in Net Assets (or Operating Surplus or Deficit). Assets are what an organization owns, or more formally, the valuable resources in an organization. They include current assets described above and long-term (or noncurrent) assets, such as land, buildings, and equipment. Liabilities are what an organization owes to others. In addition to current liabilities, there are long-term liabilities, such as long-term debts. *Net assets* are the difference between assets and liabilities. Positive net assets are often in the form of investment in an asset reserve. An asset reserve can be used to measure an organization's financial ability to withstand financial emergency. *Change in net asset* is the difference between total revenues and total expenses for the current year of an organization. It can be seen as an organizationwide operating surplus (or deficit). A positive figure indicates an increase in total net assets. A negative number eats up the asset reserve. We will come back to these concepts in Chapters 9 and 10.

Indicator 5: Fund Equity (Balance) or Fund Operating Surplus (or Deficit). Operating deficits occur when expenditures exceed revenue in the current year, which indicates that an organization consumes more than it receives. Constant recurrence of deficits exhausts an organization's reserves and puts its financial viability on the line. Deficits can occur in different funds of an organization. A fund is an accounting entity that reports its own financial assets and liabilities and fund balance. Different funds are used to record and report financial activities of different natures. For example, in a U.S. local government, the financial activities of a police department are different in nature from those of a water treatment facility. The former is considered a governmental activity while the latter is a business-type activity. They are reported in different funds—likely, the police activities in a general fund, and the water treatment activities in an enterprise fund. A fund has its own revenues and expenditures. The difference between revenues and expenditures is the *change in fund equity (balance),* which can be seen as a fund's operating surpluses (or deficits). We can choose to monitor deficits of a particular fund (such as a general fund). The fund operating deficit can be covered by reserve. We will discuss funds and fund-level financial statements in Chapter 11.

Indicator 6: Borrowing Capacity. Debt issuances can be used to finance capital improvement and occasionally short-term revenue shortages. However, excessive debts can cause serious financial troubles. How much debt is too much? One indicator that assesses an organization's debt capacity is to compare debt with total assets: the *debt ratio* (Total Debts/Total Assets). The larger the debt ratio, the lower the debt capacity. Some literature suggests that the debt ratio should not exceed a benchmark of 0.5.

Financial results indicators evaluate how efficiently an organization uses its financial resources and how effectively it produces revenues, earnings, or profits for its operation. Indicators 7 and 8, described below, are in this category.

Indicator 7: Asset Allocation Efficiency. One such indicator is *total asset turnover* (Total Revenues/Total Assets), which calculates revenue per dollar of assets. It is an indicator of asset allocation efficiency. For example, a value of 1.2 shows that every dollar in assets brings $1.2 in revenue. A higher value indicates more efficient asset allocation, as measured by higher revenue earning potential. Another similar indicator, *fixed asset turnover* (Total Revenue/Total Fixed Assets), computes revenue per dollar of assets invested in long-term assets such as equipment and properties. This ratio concerns the efficiency of fixed asset allocation. A higher ratio suggests a more efficient allocation of fixed assets.

Indicator 8: Indicators of Earning and Profitability. Earnings and profits are not objectives of many public service organizations. Nevertheless, some functions in these organizations produce business-type goods and services that should be evaluated using earnings or profitability. One such indicator is *return on assets* (Change in Net Assets/ Total Assets), which evaluates earnings per dollar of assets. For example, a value of 0.50 indicates that 50 cents of earnings are made for each dollar spent on assets. A higher value of this ratio suggests a higher earning capacity and higher profitability. Notice that a negative *change in net assets* leads to a negative ratio, which shows net asset loss per dollar of assets. A similar indicator is *return on net assets* (Change in Net Assets/Net Assets), which assesses the profitability of net assets.

What Indicators Should Be Monitored?

Because there are numerous indicators available for monitoring, using all of them would be too costly and time consuming. Selection of limited indicators is necessary. Consider the following four criteria in the selection.

First, indicators selected should meet monitoring objectives. To ensure zero deficits, operating deficits and levels of revenues and expenditures should be monitored. To ensure availability of sufficient cash to meet obligations, liquidity ratios should be monitored. If we are concerned about the possibility of resource waste in operations, indicators of asset allocation efficiency should be monitored. Oftentimes, deficit compliance, liquidity, and asset allocation efficiency are three major monitoring objectives. Other monitoring objectives include enhanced borrowing capacity and increased profitability.

Second, indicators selected should address specific monitoring needs. A surge in inventory might indicate a need to improve an organization's inventory management. A monitoring of the inventory level becomes necessary. Consistent complaints from citizens or elected officials about the increase of a specific tax point out a need to monitor the tax base and tax rate.

Third, indicators selected should meet the requirement of *monitoring frequency.* Data for some indicators may not be available frequently enough to meet the requirement of monitoring. Many tax bases and tax rates are changed annually, which does not meet the requirement of a monthly monitoring. Finally, costs associated with data collection should be acceptable. Costs are lower for indicators that exist in the current reporting system and are readily available for use; cost are higher for new indicators that require effort to collect.

Where Are the Data?

Budgets and financial reports, including the Comprehensive Annual Financial Report (CAFR) of U.S. state and local governments, are good sources for annual data. Information on assets, liabilities, fund finances, and cash flows can be found in CAFRs. CAFRs should also present demographic information in the "Statistical Section." A well-documented budget should include itemized revenues and expenditure data, information on spending efficiency and effectiveness, and the historical information that demonstrates the trends of these data. Monthly or quarterly data may be found in a financial division's internal reports or financial record books or accounting documents (i.e., accounting ledgers). Unless required by law, information at this level of detail is usually not presented in budgets or CAFRs. Efforts need to be made to retrieve this information in a standardized and systematic way in order to be included in a monitoring system.

Detecting Unacceptable Performance

This part of a monitoring system detects performance that is out of an acceptable range, or shows a deteriorating trend. A common detecting scheme consists of three major steps that include (1) examining indicators, (2) detecting the performance trend, and (3) developing a complete picture of performance.

Examining Indicators

The first step is to find out whether a financial indicator is within an acceptable performance range. To do that, the actual performance of the indicator should be compared with some form of performance standards or benchmarks, such as budgeted amounts, state- or nationwide averages, or performance of similar organizations.

Let us say that we examine this year's CAFR, and realize that there is a general fund operating deficit (the amount that total expenditures exceeded total revenue) of $150,000. The deficit is covered by our financial reserve cumulated over years. We have sufficient reserves. But large and continual deficits would eat up our reserves (assuming borrowing is too costly). To detect whether this deficit is within our acceptable range, we should compare this deficit with our budget figure. Suppose that we had expected a $300,000 surplus in our budget. The difference between the budget and the actual is –$450,000 (–150,000 – 300,000). The negative sign indicates unacceptable performance.

After detecting unacceptable performance, we should look into the possible cause of the underperformance. If the investigation uncovers a random error, for example, a once-a-decade purchase of land, then we should move on. If we find that a systematic error—one that will recur, such as increased personnel cost—is the cause of the deficit, then a strategy should be developed to deal with the deficit. A strategy may include efforts to increase revenues and to reduce expenses, or modify budget projections. Finding causes and taking actions is the subject of a later discussion in this chapter.

Detecting the Performance Trend

Regardless of whether performance is acceptable or not, it is a good idea to look into the performance trend. The second step of performance detection involves a study of the trend of the indicator. A trend will tell us whether unacceptable performance is now recurring, so that the possibility for long-term deterioration is identified, or, if the current performance is within an acceptable range, whether it is a continuation of a historical trend. In other words, a trend can show a sign of deteriorating, improving, or stable performance. In the above example, suppose that the data of operating surplus (deficits) for the past three years is shown in Table 7.1.

Table 7.1

Operating Surplus (or Deficit) of the Past Three Years ($)

	Current year	Last year	Two years ago
Actual	−150,000	−100,000	100,000
Budget	300,000	200,000	150,000
Difference	−450,000	−300,000	−50,000

Clearly, the trend indicates an increase in a negative actual–budget gap, suggesting a deteriorating performance trend for the past three years. The actual–budget gap increased by 900 percent (−$450,000/−$50,000) over the last three years. This finding indicates a stronger need for improvement than single-year data suggests.

Developing a Complete Picture of Performance

In this step, a more complete picture of performance is developed. This step is particularly important when a negative performance trend is detected. It helps us further understand *what* went wrong. It can also be seen as a prelude in understanding *why* it went wrong. This step involves the examination of other indicators that are associated with the initial indicator. In our example, because the deficit is the difference between revenues and expenditures, an examination of the revenues and expenditures should provide us with more information about the causes of the deficit.

The deficit can be a result of an unexpected revenue shortfall, overspending, or both. Table 7.2 shows that $100,000 more revenues were collected than expected, so a revenue shortfall can be ruled out. The data show that $550,000 in overspending caused the deficit. They also show that the current year's deficit is $150,000/$5,000,000 = 3.0 percent of actual revenue, which measures the relative size of the deficit. Revenue and expenditure data for the previous two years can also be analyzed in the same fashion.

Understanding the Causes and Taking Action

Not all underperformance deserves meticulous analysis. Variations from expected performance may be the result of a random event that has little chance of recurring. Or, underperformance may be caused by measurement inconsistency, such as a change in the data collection method or definition of an indicator. Random errors, such as typos in data entry, also occur. At other times, the amount of underperformance is just too small to warrant any significant investment in investigation. We are not concerned here with cases of underperformance that are caused by random or insignificant events, but will rather examine

Table 7.2

Revenues, Expenditures, and Surplus (Deficit) in the Current Year ($)

	Actual	Budget	Difference
Total revenues	5,000,000	4,900,000	100,000
Total expenditures	5,150,000	4,600,000	−550,000
Surplus or deficit	−150,000	300,000	−450,000

Table 7.3

Expenditure by Function ($)

	Actual	Budget	Difference
Personnel	2,900,000	2,500,000	−400,000
Operating	1,100,000	1,000,000	−100,000
Capital	1,150,000	1,100,000	−50,000
Total	5,150,000	4,600,000	−550,000

underperformance that results from recurring fiscal or economic conditions or systematic practices of poor planning or inefficient operation.

Using the budget deficit example above, the initial observation indicates overspending of $550,000. A further analysis, shown in Table 7.3, indicates that 73 percent (−$400,000/−$550,000) of overspending was caused by overspending on personnel. After interviewing the human resource director, it was revealed that there was a significant increase in the insurance cost for employees.

Data suggest that insurance premiums have increased over the past three years and that this increase was largely responsible for the budget deficits for the past two years. Clearly, the increase was not considered in the planning and budgeting process. If an increase is predicted for next year, the budget should be adjusted to consider such increases.

In general, except for random factors, underperformance can have three causes: unpredictable socioeconomic changes, poor planning, and/or inefficient or ineffective practices in management or operations. Budget deficits caused by lack of efforts in revenue collection or deteriorating employee productivity belong to the last category. Consequently, several approaches can be developed to deal with such underperformance. First, financial goals, objectives, or standards can be modified to reflect reality in the planning process. Second, efforts can be made to modify organizational strategies, procedures, and activities to improve efficiency and effectiveness in management or operations. Last, invalid or unreliable indicators can be deleted from the monitoring system. Unrealistic performance standards should be revised.

A Case Study

Linda Ellis is the finance director of Doreen County, Nevada. The county has a population of 312,000, with total projected revenues of $308 million this year. Although the largest revenue item is property tax (about 35 percent of the total revenue), the county has seen an increase in service charges, which are about 16 percent of total revenues. Part of this increase is due to the county's policy that, "wherever possible, the county shall institute user charges for programs and activities in the County." The county also has a fiscal policy of "keeping a prudent level of financial reserves for future unexpected expenses and revenue declines." The county has always tried to set apart 3 to 5 percent of appropriations for contingency.

The finance department has a financial monitoring system in place. The system monitors all major financial indicators. Nevertheless, Linda's monthly monitoring focuses on a very limited number of indicators of liquidity and fund balance. She believes that having sufficient cash and cash equivalents on hand is important and she also knows that it is impossible to follow all indicators closely, as the county's resources for record keeping are limited and only the most important indicators are available on a monthly basis. Most other indicators are examined during an annual review. In a recent monitoring analysis, Linda used the following steps.

Step 1: Determining and Accessing Individual Financial Indicators

One liquidity indicator Linda reviews monthly is the current ratio (Current Assets/Current Liabilities). The current ratio indicates the short-term assets available to pay short-term liabilities. For example, a ratio of 2.0 indicates that there are $2 in current assets for every dollar of the current liabilities. She uses a benchmark of 2.0, and any ratio lower than that number is a warning sign that indicates the county may not have sufficient liquidity.

In addition to the current ratio, Linda also reviews different current assets for possible troubles in asset allocation that could lead to liquidity problems. The county's current assets include cash, short-term investments, receivables, and inventories. In a recent monthly monitoring analysis, Linda noticed a steady increase in the "receivables" account, which indicates an increase in what others owe the county. "Receivables" are a current asset account that typically represents amounts due to the county within 60 days. Although an increase doesn't negatively affect the current ratio, it does indicate a slowed pace of cash inflow. In other words, the more money people owe to you, the less cash you have. Because the increase in "receivables" suggests slowed cash inflow and a possible problem in payment collection, Linda's alert was up when she noticed the increase.

Step 2: Detecting Unacceptable Performance

The latest monthly report showed a 5 percent increase in "receivables" over the last month's figure. Linda thought that it was okay if this was just a one-time increase that was caused by some customers' delayed payments. However, if the increase had been continuing over time, that would be a problem. She knew that she needed to look at past data to make a determination.

Linda reviewed the monthly averages of the "receivables" account for the past six months. To adjust the seasonal impact, she also reviewed data for the same month for the past five years. The data showed a clear trend of increase. For example, the percentage of "receivables" in the current assets increased from 12 percent to 16 percent over the last five years in the month of July. A similar increase occurred in most of the other months.

At the same time, Linda noticed a slight decrease in the cash balance. For example, cash was 59 percent of all current assets five years ago at the end of July, but was now 56 percent—a 3 percent decrease over the last five years. To determine that the decrease was caused by the "receivables" increase, Linda analyzed the data of other current assets and found that little change had occurred in them over the past five years. After consulting with two financial specialists on this matter, her final conclusion was that the decline in cash balance was largely due to the increase in "receivables."

Step 3: Understanding Causes of Underperformance

The average monthly balance of current assets is $336,000,000 for the past six months. A 3 percent decrease in cash balance indicates a decrease of $10,080,000 ($336,000,000 × 3 percent) in cash, and with an annual interest rate of 4 percent for the safest investment instruments, like treasury bills, this decrease represents an interest income loss of $403,200 ($10,080,000 × 4 percent) this year.

This would be a significant loss to the county. Linda decided to investigate the causes of the "receivables" increase. She focused on the two largest revenue resources—property taxes and user charges. No significant payment discrepancy was found for the property taxes. Most taxes were paid on time. When analyzing the payment collection for the user charges, Linda noticed a large and increasing amount in delayed payment for the county's water and sewer services. She called the public utility director and was told that an outdated address database was responsible for that. Apparently, the old database had not been updated for the past several years as the result of the budget cut. The database included many old addresses, and payment notices to these addresses were often returned. The public utility director estimated that the address error rate was about 5 percent, which was much higher than a 1 percent benchmark established by the county. The director also told Linda that the county commission had noticed the problem, and he invited Linda to attend the next commission meeting, in which the billing address database was an issue on the agenda.

Step 4: Developing a Monitoring Report

Linda agreed to attend the commission meeting. She is preparing a monitoring report that will be presented at the meeting. In the report, she plans to present the monitoring results and causes of the problem. In conclusion, she suggests an immediate update of the address database, and the establishment of multiple bill payment methods, including mail, the Internet, and in-person payments, for convenience and speed of payment.

Exercises

1. Key Terms

Purposes of financial performance monitoring
Three elements in financial monitoring
Financial indicators
Nonfinancial indicators
Financial input indicators
Total revenue
Revenue per capita
Total expenditures
Expenditures per capita
Financial process indicators
Liquidity
Current ratio
Current assets
Current liabilities
Net assets
Changes in net assets
Long-term (or noncurrent) assets
Liabilities
Asset reserves

Fund equity (balance)
Fund operating surplus (or deficit)
Funds
General fund
Enterprise funds
Debt ratio
Financial results indicators
Total asset turnover
Fixed asset turnover
Return on assets
Return on net assets
Comprehensive Annual Financial Report (CAFR)
Three steps in detecting unacceptable performance

2. Obtaining Information from the CAFR

The CAFR typically has three sections: an introduction, a financial section, and a statistical section. The financial section is the most important section in the CAFR. It includes a "Management Discussion and Analysis" (MD&A), which gives a description of a jurisdiction's financial policies and significant changes in financial conditions over the previous year. This section also includes a list of financial statements that are used to reveal financial conditions and financial performances of the jurisdiction. Most of the financial indicators discussed in this chapter can be found in these statements.

The first two statements in the financial section are the Statement of Net Assets and Statement of Activities. They are organizationwide statements, presenting financial information for a whole organization. Use a CAFR to obtain the following indicators:

1. Total assets for the primary entity in the Statement of Net Assets.
2. Total net assets for the primary entity in the Statement of Net Assets.
3. Total revenue for the primary entity in the Statement of Activities (general revenues plus program revenues).
4. Total expenses for the primary entity in the Statement of Activities.
5. Change in net assets for the primary entity in the Statement of Activities.
6. Current assets for the primary entity in the Statement of Net Assets (Total Assets – Noncurrent or Capital Assets).
7. Total liabilities for the primary entity in the Statement of Net Assets.
8. Current liabilities for the primary entity in the Statement of Net Assets (Total Liabilities – Noncurrent or Long-Term Liabilities).

3. Calculation of Financial Indicators

Use the information in the above question to compute the following financial indicators. Discuss briefly the meaning of each indicator.

1. Total revenue per resident. (Note: To find out the population figure, you may want to check the "Statistical Section" of CAFR, call the organization, or search the Web.)
2. Total expenditure per resident.
3. The current ratio.
4. The net asset ratio. (Change in Net Assets/Net Assets.)
5. Total asset turnover.
6. Fixed asset turnover. (Sometimes fixed assets are listed as "long-term assets," "noncurrent assets," or "capital assets.")
7. Return on assets.

4. Historical Comparison of the Indicators

Make an effort to obtain CAFRs for the past three years, and compare the indicators in Questions 2 and 3 over time. Report your monitoring findings.

CHAPTER 8

Cash Management

Determining the Optimal Cash Balance

Learning Objectives

After studying this chapter, you should be able to

- Develop a cash budget
- Determine an optimal cash balance
- Use the optimal cash balance in cash management decision making

There are three objectives in cash management. *Cash safety* refers to the prevention of loss of cash as the result of poor decision making or criminal behavior in cash collection, disbursement, investment, and other cash handling practices. The other two objectives are *liquidity* and *investment return*. A good cash manager maintains a sufficient amount of cash to meet financial obligations and also earns a large return through investment. These two objectives often contradict each other. Because a high level of liquidity requires readily available cash that could otherwise be invested, higher liquidity often means less investment and therefore less investment return. On the other hand, investing a large amount of cash in the market in order to achieve a good return can compromise liquidity. In fact, a fundamental challenge in cash management is to seek an *optimal cash balance* that meets the daily demand for cash, and earns a large investment return. Determination of the optimal cash balance is the focus of this chapter.

To understand the concept of optimal cash balance, think of your own personal finances. If you have a daily cash income of $500, daily cash spending of $200, and a balance of $10,000 cash in hand, you keep too much cash. You are better off investing some of the $10,000. On the other hand, if you only keep $200 cash in your pocket, you are at risk of running out of cash. So you want to find a cash balance somewhere between $200 and $10,000 that provides you with sufficient cash for daily spending and, at the same time, earns you a good investment return.

Table 8.1

Expected Cash Receipts by Source in January ($)

Sources	Amount
Property taxes	200,000
Sales taxes	100,000
Licenses and permits	50,000
Fines and forfeits	50,000
Total	400,000

Concepts and the Tool

Creating a Cash Budget

The first step to determine the optimal cash balance is to create a *cash budget* that includes future *cash receipts* and *cash disbursements*. The idea is that if cash revenues and cash spending for a given time are known, then how much or how little is left for investment is known. Table 8.1 shows the sources of future cash receipts in a local government. Monthly cash receipts are forecast.

Effective cash collection is important in managing cash receipts. The objective of cash collection is to get the cash as quickly as possible and to keep it as long as possible in order to increase liquidity or investment earnings. Consider the following approaches to facilitate cash collection.

- Providing multiple payment methods, such as pay in person, pay by mail, and electronic transfer.
- Ensuring correct addresses by updating the address database and correcting wrong addresses.
- Establishing policies for late payments.
- Using return envelopes addressed directly to a bank *lockbox* to reduce travel time of payments.
- Focusing on the payment speed of major taxpayers, service users, and large revenue sources.
- Having a customer service hotline to answer account balance questions.

Cash disbursements are results of receiving or prepaying services or products. Table 8.2 shows the cash disbursement plan in the above local government. Monthly disbursements by disbursement functions are forecast in the plan.

The objective of cash disbursement management is to hold on to cash as long as possible. A cash payment should be made only when it is necessary

Table 8.2

Expected Cash Disbursements by Function in January

Function	Amount ($)
Personnel services	250,000
Operating expenses	50,000
Capital outlays	50,000
Total	350,000

Table 8.3

Cash Budget ($)

	January	February	March	. . .
Balance on the first of the month	50,000	100,000	. . .	
Expected receipts	400,000	. . .	. . .	
Cash available	450,000	. . .	. . .	
Expected disbursements	350,000	. . .	. . .	
Balance at the end of the month	100,000	. . .	. . .	

Note: ". . ." represents any possible hypothetical figures.

and at the last possible moment without penalty for the late payment. Consider the following approaches in managing cash disbursements.

- Keeping the payment deadline in mind.
- Considering payment travel days in the mail.
- Making sure the addresses are correct.
- Calling to ensure receipt of the payments.
- Using secure electronic payment modes to improve payment speed.

After the forecast of cash receipts and disbursements is completed, a cash budget can be created. Table 8.3 illustrates a cash budget that combines monthly cash receipts and disbursements of the above local government. It also includes the *cash balance,* which is what is left in an organization's cash account at the end of the month. Monthly forecasts of cash for the rest of the year should be made to complete the table.

Clearly, creation of a cash budget requires the forecast of cash flows of revenues and expenses. Cash flows in the past can be used in the forecast. Nevertheless, accurate forecasting of cash flows is difficult, as numerous socioeconomic, demographic, and organizational factors could potentially affect cash flows. The revenue forecasting techniques introduced in Chapter 1 can be used in forecasting cash flows as well.

After a cash budget is completed and the cash balance is determined, an *investment plan* should be developed. An investment plan should include investment types, investment amounts, and the duration of investments. Safety is always a major consideration in investing public dollars. *Low-risk investments* such as U.S. federal government debts and other guaranteed securities should be favorite investment instruments in state and local governments. Short-term (within twelve months) investments include bank savings accounts, certificates of deposit (CDs), federal treasury bills, and money market mutual funds. Long-term investments (maturity > twelve months) include U.S. treasury notes and bonds, corporate bonds, and common stocks. In general, the safer the instrument, the lower the investment return.

Determining the Optimal Cash Balance

How much cash should be invested? An experienced cash manager's judgment is often as good as any quantitative model. Managers' intuition and judgment are often good predictors of cash inflows (receipts) and outflows (disbursements), and therefore the cash balance. However, some quantitative models, such as the *Miller-Orr model* can provide insights about managing cash balances and developing effective cash management strategies.

Compared with other models, such as the Economic Ordering Quantity (EOQ), the Miller-Orr model is more flexible in dealing with fluctuating cash flows and balances. The model determines a cash balance interval that includes a low cash limit—a point where the cash balance is too low— and an upper cash limit—an indication that the cash balance is too high. A return point is used to help managers make investment or cash replenishment (liquidity) decisions. The graph (Figure 8.1) shows how the Miller-Orr model works.

The *lower limit* (or minimum cash balance) could be from zero to any number deemed to be the minimum cash amount. The *upper limit* is the point at which the cash balance is more than sufficient and part of the cash should be invested. If the distance between the lower limit and the upper limit is defined as the *spread,* then Upper Limit = Lower Limit + Spread, and the spread can be derived from the following equation.

$$Spread = 3 \times \left(\frac{0.75 \times B \times V}{I} \right)^{1/3}$$

B is the transaction cost. *V* is the variance of daily net cash flow. *I* is the daily interest rate. $()^{1/3}$ is the cube root for the arithmetic in the (). The transaction cost (*B*) is the cost per transaction to covert cash to securities or vice versa. If a broker is hired, the commission (brokerage) should be included in

Figure 8.1 **The Miller-Orr Model**

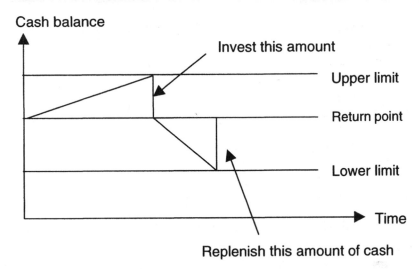

the transaction cost. Rather than hiring an external broker, an organization could choose to manage its cash internally by using its own personnel, and then the transaction cost is the cost associated with the hire and use of these people. Daily interest rate (I) is the daily rate of return on an investment. In public organizations, where safety is a major concern for investment, the interest rate for U.S. treasury bills, one of the safest investment choices, can be used.

The variance of daily net cash flow (V) is used to measure the fluctuation of cash balance. A larger value of V indicates that a cash flow fluctuates more. It can be calculated by using daily net cash flow (Daily Deposits – Daily Withdrawals) for a selected number of days (e.g., 100 days), and by computing the variance of the cash flow for these days. It is important to note that the selection of these days should reflect the true fluctuation of cash flows for an organization at a given time (e.g., a year). If the organization has different patterns of cash flows in different seasons of a year, then the days selected should include days in different seasons. Let us first look at a simple example to illustrate what the variance is, and then use Excel in the calculation. Let us say that, during the past five days, we have a series of net cash flows of $10.00 in Day 1, $20.00 in Day 2, –$5.00 in Day 3, $7.00 in Day 4, and –$10.00 in Day 5. The five-day average is ($10.00 + $20.00 – $5.00 + $7.00 – $10.00)/5 = $4.40. Table 8.4 includes the statistics needed to compute the variance.

The total of the difference squared is 31.36 + 243.36 + 88.36 + 6.76 + 207.36 = $577.20. Variance is $577.20/4 = $144.30, where 4 is the number

Table 8.4

An Example of Computing Variance of Daily Net Cash Flow

Day	Net cash flow ($) (1)	Average (2)	Difference (3) = (1) – (2)	Difference squared Square of (3)
1	10.00	4.40	5.60	31.36
2	20.00	4.40	15.60	243.36
3	–5.00	4.40	–9.40	88.36
4	7.00	4.40	2.60	6.76
5	–10.00	4.40	–10.44	207.36

of days minus 1 (5 – 1). Statisticians use the following formula to compute the variance.

$$V = \frac{\sum_{i=1}^{n}(X_i - \mu)^2}{(n-1)}$$

Xi represents individual cases (like $10.00, $20.00, . . ., in the example), where i is the representation of the individual case number. For example, X_1 is individual Case 1; X_2 is individual Case 2. μ is the average. In our example, it is $4.40. So $(Xi - \mu)$ is the difference between an individual case and the average. Σ is the summation sign used to calculate the sum of $(Xi - \mu)^2$, which is $577.20 in this example. Finally, n is the number of cases. The variance can be easily calculated from Excel's "Data Analysis Function."

Step 1: Enter the data in an Excel file.
Step 2: Go to "Data Analysis" under the "Tool" function.
Step 3: Select "Descriptive Statistics" from the "Data Analysis" window.
Step 4: Select the data for the "Input Range" of the "Descriptive Statistics" window.
Step 5: Select an "Output Range" cell located differently from the "Input Range."
Step 6: Click "Summary Statistics" and OK and you will see results shown in Excel Screen 8.1.

Use the data in Table 8.4 to practice the Excel Data Analysis. You should be able to determine the variance shown in Screen 8.1. To make cash balance decisions, you also need *the return point,* which is the cash balance point that indicates the amount of the transfer.

Excel Screen 8.1   **Calculating Variance of Net Cash Flow**

Return Point = Lower Limit + (Spread/3).

The decision rules in the Miller-Orr model are: (1) No transaction is needed if the cash balance falls between the lower limit and the upper limit. (2) If the cash balance rises to the upper limit, invest cash by the amount of Upper Limit − Return Point. (3) If the cash balance falls to the lower limit, sell investments by the amount of Return Point − Lower Limit to replenish cash. (Review Figure 8.1 to visualize this decision-making process.)

Let us look at an example. Suppose that an agency has a minimum cash balance of $20,000 (lower limit) required by its bank. Suppose that the variance of daily net cash flows is $6,250,000, a daily interest rate is 0.025 percent, and the transaction cost is $20. So, the spread = $3 \times (0.75 \times 20 \times 6,250,000/0.00025)^{1/3}$ = $21,600. Lower limit = $20,000. Upper limit = $20,000 + $21,600 = $41,600. Return point = $20,000 + ($21,600/3) = $27,200.

Thus, the agency does not need to do anything if its cash balance fluctuates between $20,000 and $41,600. Nevertheless, if the cash balance rises to $41,600, it should invest the cash in the amount of $41,600 − $27,200 = $14,400; if the cash balance falls to $20,000, it should sell $27,200 − $20,000 = $7,200 of investment instruments to replenish cash.

A word of caution is warranted here. A cash manager should always use his or her experience, and combine it with a rational way of thinking in determining the optimal cash balance. The Miller-Orr model provides such a way of thinking, but it should not replace human judgment based on careful observation of cash flow history. Also, the Miller-Orr model should be used on a trial-and-error basis before it can be fully integrated into a cash management and investment strategy. Finally, it is always a good practice to modify the strategy by frequently calculating new lower and upper limits to accommodate changes of cash flows.

A Case Study

William Jackson is finance director of Riverside, a city of 64,560 residents. The city experienced tremendous revenue growth during the last decade due to a flourishing local economy and a growing population. However, for the past two years, there have been signs of a slowdown in revenue growth. On the other hand, the population growth has already created a large demand for city services. William and his financial staff are required to explore every possible means to increase revenues. At a recent Government Finance Officers Association (GFOA) annual conference, William attended a panel in which a speaker talked about various investment strategies used in local governments across the country.

William has noticed the trend of using external markets to earn investment incomes to offset the impact of revenue decline. He has long thought about changing the investment strategies of his own city. Riverside invests its cash in a state investment pool that meets the cash needs of participant governments. The pool is like a bank that allows a participant government to borrow. The pool also guarantees a safe return of the city's cash with interest. Nevertheless, the interest rate is lower than a comparable market return. What is unclear is how much more income the city can make if it decides to use the market instead of the cash pool. Is it worth the try? To determine a possible market return for the investment of the city's cash, William did the following analysis.

Step 1: Data Collection and a Review of the Data

William first forecast cash flows for the next year. His forecast was largely determined using last year's cash flows with minor modifications based on assumptions of next year's financial condition. Table 8.5 presents monthly

Table 8.5

Cash Flows and Balances of Riverside (%)

	Cash balance on the 1st	Receipts	Disburse-ments	Net cash flow in the month
January	22,437,583	1,680,014	3,609,873	−1,929,859
February	20,507,724	1,683,064	818,270	864,794
March	21,372,518	1,113,609	1,828,521	−714,912
April	20,657,606	1,606,122	2,051,595	−445,473
May	20,212,133	1,326,972	986,256	340,716
June	20,552,849	983,573	2,979,870	−1,996,297
July	16,187,359	153,870	1,094,120	−940,250
August	15,247,109	1,254,447	810,883	443,564
September	15,690,673	511,129	629,332	−118,203
October	15,572,470	1,562,141	2,660,760	−1,098,619
November	14,473,851	870,592	625,471	245,121
Dcember	14,718,972	12,216,997	4,498,386	7,718,611
Monthly average	18,135,904	2,080,211	1,882,778	197,433

forecasts of cash receipts, disbursements, and cash balances for the next year.

The data show that the city has an average monthly cash balance of $18,135,904, an average monthly cash receipt of $2,080,211, an average monthly disbursement of $1,882,778, and an average monthly net cash flow of $2,080,211 − $1,882,778 = $197,433. A closer look at the data shows cash receipts surged in December, when the city's property tax bills were due. Accordingly, the cash balance surged in January and then decreased every month until the next January. So, more cash should be available for investment after the New Year and the amount declines gradually throughout the year.

Step 2: Use of the Miller-Orr Model

But William still needs to know exactly how much cash can be invested. First, he decided to keep a minimum cash balance of $3,000,000. His logic was that the figure should cover the average monthly withdrawals, $1,882,778, and a minimum balance of $1,000,000 in a bank for free banking services. This is the lower limit in the Miller-Orr model, and any balance lower than this is considered too low.

To calculate the variance of daily net cash flow, William first used Excel to determine the variance of monthly net cash flow, $6,432,190,674,028. Notice that Excel calls it "sample variance." Because this is such a large number, Excel may present a 6.43219 E + 12, which means twelve zeros after the decimal. For calculation purposes, a proximate number, 6,432,190,000,000, can be used. This is the *monthly* net cash flow. To get the daily net cash flow, William divided it by thirty days of a month to arrive at $6,432,190,674,028/30 = $214,406,355,801.

To calculate the interest rate, William weighed the safety of his investment very heavily, so he chose a short-term rate of federal treasury bills as the benchmark, which paid an annual interest of 5 percent at the time. The daily interest rate is .05/365 = 0.000137. Also, the city uses an investment broker who charges a $200 fee for each transaction. According to the Miller-Orr model, the cash spread = $3 \times (0.75 \times $200 \times 214,406,355,801/0.000137)^{1/3}$ = $1,850,649. Therefore, the upper limit is $3,000,000 + $1,850,649 = $4,850,649. The return point is $3,000,000 + $1,850,649/3 = $3,616,883.

Step 3: Conducting the Analysis

Several things became clear to William after the analysis. First, the city does not want to have a cash balance lower than $3.0 million. However, keeping a balance of about $4.8 million (the upper limit) appears to be sufficient to meet the cash demand of the city. The city's current cash balance, an average of about $18.0 million, is simply too high. Second, if the city keeps a balance of $4.8 million, it can invest $18.0 million – $4.8 million = $13.2 million. The current annual interest rate in the state investment pool is 4 percent. So the annual investment income in the state pool is $13.2 million $\times$ 4 percent = $528,000. In comparison, if the city invests in the federal treasury bills that pay 5 percent interest annually, it can make $13.2 million $\times$ 5 percent = $660,000 annually in interest. That is $660,000 – $528,000 = $132,000 more than the investment earning in the state cash pool. Third, of course, the above analysis is based on estimated cash flows that may change. Significant socioeconomic, organizational, or policy changes could lead to fluctuation in revenues and expenditures and thus changes in cash flows and cash balances.

Step 4: Making Decisions

Based on the results of the Miller-Orr model and the above analysis, William proposed the following cash management strategy. First, the city should consider withdrawing from the state cash pool, or at least gradually reducing its investment in the pool. Second, the city should reduce its cash balance to $3,616,883, the return point, and invest the cash in ninety-day federal treasury bills. If the cash balance reaches $4,850,649, the city should invest $4,850,649 − $3,616,883 = $1,233,766 in the market (likely in federal treasury bills); if the cash balance falls below $3,000,000, the city should sell $3,616,883 − $3,000,000 = $616,883 in investments to obtain needed cash. Finally, the city should closely monitor the daily cash balance in order to detect possible liquidity problems. The city should also conduct a thorough review of its cash management and investment strategy every year.

Exercises

1. Key Terms

Cash safety
Liquidity
Investment returns
Cash budget
Cash receipts
Cash disbursements
Cash balance
Optimal cash balance
Investment plans
Low-risk investments
Miller-Orr model
Lower limit
Upper limit
Spread
Return point
Transaction cost
Daily interest rate
Net cash flows
Variance of daily net cash flows
Decision rules in the Miller-Orr model

2. Calculations

Table 8.6 consists of cash flow data for a selected ten days.

1. Calculate the variance of net daily cash flows.
2. Assuming a lower limit of $200, a transaction cost of $10, and an annual interest rate of 10 percent, what is the upper limit and what is the return point using the Miller-Orr model?

Table 8.6

Cash Flows of Selected Days ($)

Day	Receipts	Disbursement
1	50	70
2	90	40
3	80	80
4	100	120
5	70	140
6	50	50
7	80	40
8	130	110
9	60	100
10	110	80

Table 8.7

Monthly Cash Flows: Bridgetown Foundation ($)

	Two years ago	Last year	Current year
Cash balance (January 1st)	610,000	1,245,000	2,016,770
Receipts	865,000	873,650	871,903
Disbursements	1,050,000	930,000	928,140
Net cash flow, January	−185,000	−56,350	−56,237
Cash balance (February 1st)	425,000	1,188,650	1,960,533
Receipts	250,000	250,500	249,999
Disbursements	240,000	240,480	239,999
Net cash flow, February	10,000	10,020	10,000
Cash balance (March 1st)	435,000	1,198,670	1,970,533
Receipts	300,000	303,000	302,394
Disbursements	280,000	282,800	282,234
Net cash flow, March	20,000	20,200	20,160
Cash balance (April 1st)	455,000	1,218,870	1,990,692
Receipts	570,000	575,700	574,549
Disbursements	325,000	328,250	327,594
Net cash flow, April	245,000	247,450	246,955
Cash balance (May 1st)	700,000	1,466,320	2,237,647
Receipts	1,096,000	1,106,960	980,500
Disbursements	320,000	323,200	945,000
Net cash flow, May	776,000	783,760	35,500
Cash balance (June 1st)	1,476,000	2,250,080	2,273,147
Receipts	134,000	135,340	135,069
Disbursements	320,000	323,200	322,554
Net cash flow, June	−186,000	−187,860	−187,484

	Two years ago	Last year	Current year
Cash balance (July 1st)	1,290,000	2,062,220	2,085,663
Receipts	280,000	282,800	282,234
Disbursements	508,000	513,080	512,054
Net cash flow, July	−228,000	−230,280	−229,819
Cash balance (August 1st)	1,062,000	1,831,940	1,855,844
Receipts	370,000	373,700	372,953
Disbursements	325,000	328,250	327,594
Net cash flow, August	45,000	45,450	45,359
Cash balance (September 1st)	1,107,000	1,877,390	1,901,203
Receipts	285,000	287,850	287,274
Disbursements	315,000	318,150	317,514
Net cash flow, September	−30,000	−30,300	−30,239
Cash balance (October 1st)	1,077,000	1,847,090	1,870,963
Receipts	270,000	272,700	272,155
Disbursements	335,000	338,350	337,673
Net cash flow, October	−65,000	−65,650	−65,519
Cash balance (November 1st)	1,012,000	1,781,440	1,805,445
Receipts	892,000	900,920	899,118
Disbursements	320,000	323,200	322,554
Net cash flow, November	572,000	577,720	576,565
Cash balance (December 1st)	1,584,000	2,359,160	2,382,009
Receipts	116,000	117,160	116,926
Disbursements	455,000	459,550	458,631
Net cash flow, December	−339,000	−342,390	−341,705
Average monthly Beginning cash balance	936,083	1,693,903	2,029,204
Receipts	452,333	456,690	445,423
Disbursements	399,417	392,376	443,462
Net cash flow	52,917	64,314	1,961

3. Cash Management in Bridgetown

You are a financial analyst in the Bridgetown Foundation—a public service agency in Chicago that provides specialized mental care services to the poor. The foundation's financial resources are mainly from various state and federal grants and business or individual donations. In a recent financial audit, an independent auditor suggested the foundation explore the possibility of investing in the market as an additional revenue source. You are assigned the responsibility of analyzing the foundation's cash flows to determine whether such a possibility exists and, if it does, how much the foundation should invest and what the investment strategy should be. You pull out the cash flow information for the last three years as shown in Table 8.7.

1. Create a cash budget for the next year. Use the proper forecasting techniques (from Chapter 1) and defend your reasoning for your choice of technique.
2. Assuming a lower limit of $1,000,000, a transaction fee of $200, and a 5 percent annual interest rate, use the Miller-Orr model to determine the upper limit and the return point of the cash balance.
3. Do you see any investment opportunities for the foundation's cash? If yes, develop an investment strategy for the foundation.

PART III

TOOLS FOR FINANCIAL REPORTING AND ANALYSIS

CHAPTER 9

Financial Reporting and Analysis

The Statement of Net Assets

Learning Objectives

After studying this chapter, you should be able to

- Understand key elements in the statement of net assets
- Understand the accounting process
- Use the information in the statement of net assets in financial analysis

Why care about financial information? There are two fundamental reasons for a manager to obtain and understand financial information. One is to use the information to make managerial and operational decisions. The manager can better plan, manage, and evaluate a service if he or she knows how much it costs, and that information can be obtained from the financial reporting system. Another reason is to demonstrate accountability by keeping stakeholders informed about the financial condition and operation of the organization. Stakeholders in government organizations or agencies include citizens, elected officials, other governments, nonprofit organizations, and businesses. They have vital interests in government finance as taxpayers, oversight bodies, evaluators, or contractors of governmental services. A manager has a responsibility to answer their questions about the organization's finances.

How is financial information reported? When a close friend asks you how are you doing financially, how do you respond? There are two ways to tell a financial story. You can reveal how much you earn, but that is not a complete financial picture, because you also spend. If you make $50,000 and spend $50,000, you save nothing. If you spend $45,000 instead, you save $5,000. So another way to report your finances is to use net worth. In the above example, where does the $5,000 in savings go? It goes to your net worth. We use the term *net worth* to measure what you possess or own after taking out what you owe. Say that you have a house, some furniture, a car, a retirement account, a bank checking account, and some cash for a total of $200,000. Your bills include a mortgage, a car loan, and other payments totaling $160,000. Your net worth is $200,000 – $160,000 = $40,000.

In finance, net worth is often called net assets. Assets are what you own, and liabilities are what you owe. The financial statement prepared to disclose these financial figures is generally called the *balance sheet*. In U.S. state and local governments, the balance sheet information for a government as a whole is reported in the *statement of net assets*. Nonprofit organizations may use the name the *statement of financial position* to disclose their balance sheet information. On the other hand, the financial statement used to report annual revenues and expenses is the *statement of activities* (or operations). Sources and uses of cash and cash equivalents are reported in the *statement of cash flows*. We focus on the statement of net assets in this chapter and the statement of activities in Chapter 10.

Concepts and the Tool

What Information Is in the Statement of Net Assets?

Obviously, what you own minus what you owe is what is left. In accounting language, "what you own" is called *assets,* "what you owe" is *liabilities,* and "what is left" is *net assets,* so

$$\text{Assets} - \text{Liabilities} = \text{Net Assets}$$

Or

$$\text{Assets} = \text{Liabilities} + \text{Net Assets}$$

This is the *fundamental accounting equation.* This equation is true regardless of the types of financial transactions that occur. Your assets are *always* equal to the sum of your liabilities and net assets. If they are not equal, an error(s) must have occurred in your accounting or reporting practices or calculation processes.

More formally, assets are defined as economic resources available and liabilities are amounts owed to outside entities and employees. It is important to note that the terms assets and liabilities are used as accounting concepts here, not in any other ways. For example, we often say a good reputation is an "asset" to an organization and a bad reputation is a "liability." But they are not accounting definitions.

What types of assets does a public organization have? Assets can be broken down into *current assets* and *noncurrent assets.* In general, current assets are cash, cash equivalents, or resources that can be converted to cash within a year or that will be consumed within a year. Noncurrent assets are long-term assets such as lands, plant, equipment, and long-term investments over a year. Note that a year is used as a division of assets into current and noncurrent assets because it represents the length of a business cycle in many governmental organizations. The following is a list of common asset accounts.

- *Cash or cash equivalents.* This category may include bank savings and checking accounts, short-term certificates of deposit, and other assets that can be converted to cash quickly and easily.
- *Investments.* This category includes marketable securities such as stocks and bonds, real estate, and other investment vehicles.
- *Accounts receivable.* When an organization provides a product to a customer and has not received the payment, the amount is reported as *receivable*, which suggests that the payment will be collected in the future. There can be many types of receivables. Examples include *property taxes receivable* and *interest and penalty receivable.*
- *Inventory.* This category is for the materials and supplies that will be used in producing goods or services.
- *Prepaid expenses (prepayment, advance payment).* These are the payments for goods or services that have not yet been received. For example, if you make an advance payment of $1,000 rent the last day of this year, but the rent will cover you for the next whole year, this $1,000 is a prepaid expense at the end of this year. Notice that long-term prepayment (more than one year) is referred as a *deferred charge* and is reported in the long-term asset section of the statement of net assets.
- *Long-term assets or fixed assets.* These assets are often in the form of land, plant, building, infrastructure, and equipment.

Liabilities represent obligations of an organization. Organizations typically have liabilities that will require payments to suppliers, employees, financial institutions, bondholders, and other governments. Like assets, a liability can be classified as a *current liability* or *noncurrent liability.* Current liabilities will be paid within a short time, often a year, while noncurrent liabilities are due beyond a year (or a business cycle). The following is a list of common liability accounts.

- *Accounts payable.* These accounts show the amount an organization owes others. There are a variety of payable accounts, such as *wage payable* and *interest payable.*

- *Long-term debts.* These could include an organization's long-term loans or leases.
- *Deferred revenue.* When an organization receives a payment for services that it has not yet provided, the payment is reported as *deferred revenue.* It is a liability. For example, suppose that a power provider receives $1,200 for a one-year service contract. At the time that the money is received, the power provider has not yet provided its service to the customer. This $1,200 is deferred revenue for the power provider. Notice that some organizations use *unearned revenues* for short-term liability and deferred revenue for long-term liability.

If an organization has more assets than liabilities, it has a positive figure in net assets. Net assets can be restricted or unrestricted. *Restricted net assets* are net assets whose use has been restricted for specified purposes or for the time of use. For example, net assets could be restricted for the purposes of paying debts. *Unrestricted net assets* are net assets whose use has not been restricted. In U.S. state and local governments, net assets information can be found in the statement of net assets—the first financial statement in CAFR. Table 9.1 presents an example of that statement in a hypothetical city of Evergreen, Florida.

The Accounting Process

Where does the information in the statement of net assets come from? Accounting is the process by which financial data are recorded, processed, and reported. In an accounting cycle, raw financial information is obtained and processed to be reported in the final statements. There are four phases in an accounting cycle, and each phase represents a step to ensure the information is accurately recorded and presented, so adherence to the accounting cycle is a means to ensure financial accountability. Below are the phases in an accounting cycle:

Evidence of Transactions → The Accounting Journal →
The Accounting Ledger → Financial Statements and Reports

Evidence of transactions can be receipts of purchases, payments, purchase orders, or anything that indicates that a transaction has occurred. These pieces of evidence are reported by either the accounting department or user departments for initial entries in the accounting system. An accounting journal is simply a chronological listing of every financial event

Table 9.1

Statement of Net Assets: The City of Evergreen, Florida, for the Year Ending December 31, 2004 ($)

Assets	
Current assets	
Cash	1,500,000
Accounts receivable	560,000
Inventory	690,000
Total current assets	2,750,000
Fixed assets	
Land	3,000,000
Equipment, net	2,000,000
Total fixed assets	5,000,000
Total assets	7,750,000
Liabilities and net assetts	
Liabilities	
Current liabilities	
Accounts payable	3,000,000
Wages payable	1,300,000
Total current liabilities	4,300,000
Long-term liabilities	
Bonds payable	1,000,000
Total liabilities	5,300,000
Net assets	
Unrestricted	1,500,000
Restricted	950,000
Total net assets	2,450,000
Total liabilities and net assets	7,750,000

that has occurred in an organization. It is similar to a diary in that events are listed in the order they occur and as concurrently as possible. A journal entry often includes the transaction description, transaction dates, related accounts, transaction amounts, and reference number. Figure 9.1 illustrates the accounting journal record for a transaction in which the city of Evergreen paid its December 2004 salaries, totaling $50,000, on January 1, 2005.

Notice that two accounts, wages payable and cash, are used to record this transaction. In fact, every accounting transaction must be recorded in at least two accounts. This accounting practice is called *double-entry accounting*. It is one way to ensure reporting trueness and accuracy.

Another accounting practice in recording transactions is the use of *debit* and *credit* balances. Use of debits and credits ensures that transactions are

Figure 9.1   **Example of an Accounting Journal**

City of Evergreen
General Journal, 2005

Reference Number	Transaction	Description	Account	Debits	Credits
001(1/1/2005)	Pay salaries	$50,000	Wages Payable	$50,000	
			Cash		$50,000
002(1/1/2005)	. . .	. . .	. . .	. . .	. . .
. . .	. . .	. . .	. . .	. . .	. . .

Note: ". . ." represents information of any possible transactions.

reported in such a fashion that they can be traced and checked according to the following equation.

$$\text{Amount Debited} = \text{Amount Credited}$$

The accounting rules of reporting transactions with debits and credits are: asset accounts are increased by debits and decreased by credits; liability and net asset accounts are increased by credits and decreased by debits. In the above example, cash is an asset account. It decreases by $50,000 because cash was used to pay the salaries. So it is credited by $50,000. Wages payable is a liability account. It decreases by $50,000 because the amount owed for salaries decreases. Therefore, we record it on the debit side. As you may have noticed, the amount debited ($50,000) is equal to the amount credited ($50,000) in this example.

The next phase in the accounting cycle is the use of the general ledger. A ledger is used to summarize and accumulate the transaction information. Unlike a journal, which is organized by dates of transactions, a ledger is arranged by account. For example, we could summarize all transaction information concerning cash under a cash ledger account. A ledger account typically contains an account name, transaction date, transaction reference numbers, debit amounts, credit amounts, and balances. Figure 9.2 shows elements of a general ledger account with the information from the Evergreen example.

The last phase in the accounting cycle is to present financial information in a set of financial statements, including the statement of net assets.

Figure 9.2   **Example of an Accounting Ledger**

City of Evergreen
General Ledger, 2005

Account 101: Cash

Reference Number	Debits	Credits	Balance
Balance 12/31/2004			$1,500,000
001 (1/1/2005)		$50,000	$1,450,000
002 . . .			
003 . . .			
. . .			
. . .			

Note: ". . ." represents the related information of other transactions.

Remember that the accounting equation is always true for any transaction. Figure 9.3 demonstrates this with the transaction in the Evergreen example. Notice that both sides of the equation decrease by $50,000, so the equation still holds true. All other transactions are recorded in a similar way, and they are summarized and reported in financial statements.

Principles that Govern Accounting Practices

Accounting practices involve recording and reporting financial information. These practices rely on accounting principles for guidance and standardization. Just like traffic signals are the same in all U.S. cities, uniform accounting principles regulate ways that financial transactions are recorded and reported. The Financial Accounting Standards Board (FASB) and the Governmental Accounting Standards Board (GASB) develop so-called Generally Accepted Accounting Principles or GAAPs. The FASB establishes accounting and reporting standards for not-for-profit and for-profit organizations, and accounting and reporting standards for state and local governments are established by GASB. GAAPs are conventions or rules in financial accounting and reporting. Here is a brief discussion of some GAAPs related to state and local governments.

Who reports? A reporting entity should be determined in any financial reporting. A *primary government* is defined as a state or local government that has a separate elected governing body and is fiscally independent of other state or local governments. Governments also use the term *component*

Figure 9.3   **The Accounting Equation with a Transaction**

$$\text{Assets} = \text{Liabilities} + \text{Net Assets}$$

Assets	=	Liabilities	+	Net Assets
Cash		Wages Payable		
–$50,000		–$50,000		

units for the entities that are legally separate from the primary government but have close financial or governing relationships with the primary government. Examples of component units include public universities, housing authorities, and retirement systems.

The concept of *monetary denominator* refers to the fact that all actions that have a financial element must be monetized. Land and inventories need to be converted to monetary terms. There is a preference to use *objective evidence and the cost conventions* in financial reporting, rather than subjective estimation. The concept of *conservatism* refers to the need to consider risk in collecting revenues and the fact that less than 100 percent of them can be collected. The *going concern* concept refers to the assumption that an organization is going to continue in business for the foreseeable future. The principle of *materiality* requires that an auditor report significant (material) reporting errors.

Finally, the *accrual* concept requires that organizations recognize all economic and financial transactions as they report their financial positions and operations. That is, revenues are recorded at the time goods and services are provided regardless of when payment is received; expenditures are recorded at the time that assets have been consumed or liabilities incurred in the process of providing goods and services. We will come back to this concept in more detail in the next chapter.

A Case Study

Joe Klein is the city manager of Evergreen in Heaven County, Florida, a city that serves about 5,000 residents. Joe was hired early this year when the previous city manager retired. The city has a police department, a parks and recreation department, a public works department, a local library, and an administrative department. It relies on the county for other local services such as fire protection, code enforcement, and health and human services.

The financial division in the administrative department prepares the city's CAFR. In the past, the previous city manager never bothered to read the document. He claimed that the CAFR was too long, included too many numbers, and confused, rather than helped, him. When he had a financial question, he called the finance director.

Joe is a firm believer that financial management is the center of governance, and that good financial management practices ensure efficient use of resources and provide a solid foundation for quality services. He is reluctant to rely completely on financial personnel for interpretation of financial information. He believes that his own analysis may tell a different story, and that with a solid knowledge of the city's finances, he will have a better idea of how to improve the city's services. To do his analysis, he first reviewed the Management Discussion and Analysis (MD&A) in the CAFR, and then put out the city's statement of net assets from the CAFR. His analysis consisted of several simple steps.

Step 1: Reviewing and Analyzing this Year's Statement of Net Assets

First, Joe calculated the percentage for each asset category in total assets as shown in Table 9.2. By doing this, he found that 19.4 percent of total assets were in cash and 35.5 percent were current assets. These numbers gave him an idea as to what assets were available. He also did the same calculation for liabilities and net assets. He found that liabilities took up a very high percentage (68.4 percent) of total liabilities and net assets, which might be a warning sign that the city's level of liabilities is too high. He was also concerned that a large amount of net assets was restricted (12.2 percent). To better understand the meaning of these numbers, Joe compared them with the numbers from the previous year.

Step 2: Comparing with Last Year's Statement

The comparison in Table 9.3 shows a few changes from the previous year that caused Joe concerns. He wrote them down in a note and planned to discuss them with the finance director.
On assets:

- Cash decreased from the previous year by $500,000. Does it pose a liquidity problem?
- Inventory increased sharply from $250,000 to $690,000—a whopping 176 percent! (($690,000 − $250,000)/$250,000). What has happened? Should we do an inventory analysis?
- The value of net equipment decreased from $2,500,000 to $2,000,000. Does this mean our equipment is aged and needs replacement soon? If so, how soon?

Table 9.2

Asset and Liability Allocations: The City of Evergreen, Florida, as of December 31, 2004

	Dollars	Percent
Current assets		
Cash	1,500,000	19.4
Accounts receivable	560,000	7.2
Inventory	690,000	8.9
Total current assets	2,750,000	35.5
Fixed assets		
Land	3,000,000	38.7
Equipment, net	2,000,000	25.8
Total fixed assets	5,000,000	64.5
Total assets	7,750,000	100.0
Liabilities		
Current liabilities		
Accounts payable	3,000,000	38.7
Wages payable	1,300,000	16.8
Total current liabilities	4,300,000	55.5
Long-term liabilities		
Bonds payable	1,000,000	12.9
Total liabilities	5,300,000	68.4
Net assets		
Unrestricted	1,500,000	19.4
Restricted	950,000	12.2
Total net assets	2,450,000	31.6
Total liabilities and net assets	7,750,000	100.0

- Total assets decreased from $8,050,000 to $7,750,000—a 3.8 percent decline. We should look at more data to see if there is a trend of total asset decline.

On liabilities and net assets:

- There was an increase in restricted net assets from $500,000 to $950,000. As the use of these net assets is restricted, an increase indicates less flexibility for the city to use these assets.
- Unrestricted net assets decreased from $2,000,000 to $1,500,000. Is there any indication that this decrease is in a trend?

Table 9.3

Statement of Net Assets Comparison: The City of Evergreen ($)

	12/31/2004	12/31/2003
Assets		
Current assets		
Cash	1,500,000	2,000,000
Accounts receivable	560,000	300,000
Inventory	690,000	250,000
Total current assets	2,750,000	2,550,000
Fixed assets		
Land	3,000,000	3,000,000
Equipment, net	2,000,000	2,500,000
Total fixed assets	5,000,000	5,500,000
Total assets	7,750,000	8,050,000
Liabilities and net assets		
Liabilities		
Current liabilities		
Accounts payable	3,000,000	3,000,000
Wages payable	1,300,000	1,050,000
Total current liabilities	4,300,000	4,050,000
Long-term liabilities		
Bonds payable	1,000,000	1,500,000
Total liabilities	5,300,000	5,550,000
Net assets		
Unrestricted	1,500,000	2,000,000
Restricted	950,000	500,000
Total net assets	2,450,000	2,500,000
Total liabilities and net assets	7,750,000	8,050,000

- There is a $50,000 decrease in net assets from $2,500,000 to $2,450,000. A closer examination of the causes of this decline is warranted.

Step 3: Searching for Solutions and Taking Actions

Joe then reviewed the CAFR to see whether his above questions were addressed. In the MD&A, the finance director attributed the total asset decline mainly to the depreciation of equipment. Nevertheless, none of Joe's other concerns were addressed in the analysis. He picked up phone to call the finance director.

Exercises

1. Key Terms

Net worth
Balance sheet
Statement of net assets
Statement of financial position
Statement of activities
Fundamental accounting equation
Assets
Liabilities
Net assets
Current assets
Noncurrent assets
Cash or cash equivalents
Investments
Accounts receivable
Inventory
Prepaid expenses
Long-term assets or fixed assets
Current liability
Noncurrent liabilities
Accounts payable
Long-term debts
Deferred revenues
Restricted net assets
Unrestricted net assets
Accounting cycle
Accounting journal
Accounting ledger
Double-entry accounting
Debit and credit
Primary government
Component units
Monetary denominator
Objective evidence
Cost convention
Conservatism
Going concern
Materiality
Accrual accounting basis

2. Financial Analysis of the CAFR

Access the CAFRs of three recent years of a government. Refer to the Statement of Net Assets to conduct an analysis on assets, liabilities, and net assets to identify any changes that cause concern about the financial condition of the government.

CHAPTER 10

Financial Reporting and Analysis

The Statement of Activities

Learning Objectives

After studying this chapter, you should be able to

- Understand key elements in the statement of activities
- Understand the concept of accounting basis
- Apply the information in the statement of activities in financial analysis

In Chapter 9, we learned how to evaluate an organization's financial condition by examining its assets, liabilities, and net assets. Now we discuss another aspect of financial condition—revenues and expenses. What is the relationship between net assets and revenues/expenses? Think of your personal finances. If your revenues are larger than your expenses (i.e., you save) for a long time, you will accumulate a large amount of wealth over time. Net assets are cumulative wealth, while revenue and expense information represents financial performance over a particular time period. A combination of both net asset and revenue/expense information provides a relatively complete picture of an organization's finances.

Concepts and the Tool

The financial statement that presents revenues and expenses is called the *statement of activities* in governmental organizations (or, the statement of operations, the income statement in many business organizations). Like the statement of net assets, the statement of activities presents the financial information for a government as a whole. Fund-level financial information (Chapter 11) is not presented in the statement of assets or the statement of activities. It is included in the fund-level financial statements, such as the balance sheet of governmental funds. The following section presents the key elements in the statement of activities and the accounting bases on which this statement is prepared.

What Information Is in the Statement of Activities?

Expenses

First, expenses are classified and presented by functions or programs. For example, a city can present expenses in the major service functions of public safety, transportation, education, health, and human services. Or it can choose to present expenses in a more detailed fashion. Public safety can be further broken down into police, fire protection, emergency rescue, corrections, and so forth. How detailed the presentation is depends on the needs of the reader and the cost of data collection. In general, expenses for different types of services should be presented. If a government also provides *business-type* services, such as water/sewer services and utility provision, then the expenses of these services should be presented separately from *governmental activities.* This separation is necessary because the expenses of business-type activities can be offset by the revenues generated from these activities, and such breakeven is not possible in most governmental activities. Additionally, if a government has component units, the expenses of component units should be presented in a separate column from expenses of the primary government.

If a government allocates overhead, interest, and other indirect expenses to *direct services,* it can also present the allocated expenses in a separate column. Direct services are those provided to customers, residents, or clients outside the government. For example, a police department provides services directly to residents, while a vehicle maintenance division of the government offers services only to other departments within the government. The expenses in the vehicle maintenance division are *indirect expenses* and can be allocated to direct services.

Table 10.1 shows how expense information can be presented. Only primary government expenses are shown. The percentage of each expense of the total is also presented. Realize that the percentage information is not reported in the actual statement of activities; you will have to calculate it by yourself.

The table shows that the largest expense item is public safety, which accounts for almost half of the total expenses. A distant second is the 14.0 percent spent on transportation, while 13.4 percent is spent on general government, which is mainly the cost of general management, planning, personnel, and financial management. Governmental activities make up 84.7 percent of spending, and 15.3 percent is spent on business-type activities.

Table 10.1

Expenses in the Statement of Activities: The City of Evergreen, Florida, for the Year Ending December 31, 2004

Functions/program	Expenses ($)	Percentage
Governmental activities		
General government	420,000	13.4
Public safety	1,500,000	47.7
Transportation	440,000	14.0
Health and human services	300,000	9.6
Total	2,660,000	84.7
Business-type activities		
Water	150,000	4.8
Sewer	210,000	6.7
Parking	120,000	3.8
Total	480,000	15.3
Total primary government	3,140,000	100.0

The percentage information is more useful when compared with percentages from past years. Percentage changes can be identified and analyzed in a historical context to demonstrate trends in spending patterns.

Revenues

The sources of revenue are presented in the statement. In governments, revenue sources include taxes, fees and charges, grants, investment earnings, and other revenue sources. In general, revenue sources can be classified into two categories: *program revenues* and *general revenues*. Revenues generated through specific functions or programs are called program revenues. For example, a city Clerk's Office could charge a fee for providing a copy of a record or document. Since the Clerk's Office performs a general government function, this fee should be presented as program revenue for the general government. Another example of program revenues is a grant contributed to a specified program or function. A grant designated for public safety is an example. It should be presented as the program revenue for public safety. The difference between program expenses and program revenues is *net (expenses) revenues*. Table 10.2 shows the presentation of net (expenses) revenues.

It should not be a surprise that governmental activities have a net expense of $2,268,000, because these services are "governmental" by nature—they are not designed to generate net revenues. On the other hand, business-type

Table 10.2

Expenses, Program Revenues, and Net (Expenses) Revenues in the Statement of Activities: The City of Evergreen, Florida, for the Year Ending December 31, 2004 ($)

Functions/program	Expenses (1)	Program revenues (2)	Net (expenses) revenues (2) − (1)
Governmental activities			
General government	420,000	140,000	(280,000)
Public safety	1,500,000	53,000	(1,447,000)
Transportation	440,000	49,000	(391,000)
Health and human services	300,000	150,000	(150,000)
Total	2,660,000	392,000	(2,268,000)
Business-type activities			
Water	150,000	180,000	30,000
Sewer	210,000	300,000	90,000
Parking	120,000	60,000	(60,000)
Total	480,000	540,000	60,000
Total primary government	3,140,000	932,000	(2,208,000)

activities produce net revenues of $60,000. Among three business-type activities, the parking service is losing money. The city has a total net expense of $2,208,000, which should be covered by general revenues.

The revenues that are not associated with specific programs or functions are called *general revenues*. General revenues include taxes, intergovernmental revenues, grants and contributions not restricted to specific programs, investment earnings, and miscellaneous revenues. General revenues should also be presented in the statement of activities. Table 10.3 is an example of such a presentation.

Total general revenues are $2,158,000, and they are $50,000 less than the net expenses of $2,208,000. As general revenues are often the largest revenue source, it is useful to identify the major sources of general revenues. In our example, property tax is 57.9 percent ($1,250,000/$2,158,000) of total general revenues. The revenue collection effort should be concentrated on this revenue.

If an organization collects revenues from a special source, they should be reported as a *special item*. The revenue from sale of public land is an example. When resources are transferred from business-type to governmental activities (or vice versa) without receiving anything in return (i.e., a subsidy), they are called *transfers*. If an organization has revenues generated from special items and transfers, it should present total general revenues, special items, and transfers in the statement of activities.

Table 10.3

Expenses, Program Revenues, Net (Expenses) Revenues, and General Revenues in the Statement of Activities: The City of Evergreen, Florida, for the Year Ending December 31, 2004 ($)

Function/Program	Expenses (1)	Program revenues (2)	Net (expenses) revenues (2) – (1)
Governmental activities			
General government	420,000	140,000	(280,000)
Public safety	1,500,000	53,000	(1,447,000)
Transportation	440,000	49,000	(391,000)
Health and human services	300,000	150,000	(150,000)
Total	2,660,000	392,000	(2,268,000)
Business-type activities			
Water	150,000	180,000	30,000
Sewer	210,000	300,000	90,000
Parking	120,000	60,000	(60,000)
Total	480,000	540,000	60,000
Total primary government	3,140,000	932,000	(2,208,000)
General revenues			
Taxes			
Property taxes			1,250,000
Sales taxes			320,000
Franchise taxes			230,000
Grants not restricted for specific programs			260,000
Investment earnings			43,000
Miscellaneous			55,000
Total general revenues			2,158,000
Change in net assets			(50,000)
Net assets—beginning			2,500,000
Net assets—ending			2,450,000

Change in Net Assets

The $50,000 difference between general revenues and net expenses is called *change in net assets*. In fact, the $50,000 is the difference between total revenues (program revenues and general revenues) and total expenses ($932,000 + $2,158,000 – $3,140,000). Table 10.3 shows this figure and net assets at the beginning and the end of the year. The balance of net assets is $2,500,000 at the beginning of 2004 (see Table 9.3 on p. 125 for the source of this figure). The balance decreases by $50,000 to $2,450,000 at the end of 2004 as the result of the $50,000 net expenses in operations. As discussed in Chapter 7 on financial performance monitoring, change in net assets is a measure of financial results. A decline of $50,000 in net assets shows that the city's financial condition is worse than it was at the beginning of the year by this measure.

Accounting Bases

Suppose that you are a car dealer and you sold a car for $50,000 today, but the payment won't be collected until next year. Do you count the $50,000 as revenue in this year or next year? If you report the revenue in a period when it occurs, regardless of the payment status, you are using *accrual basis* accounting. If you record the revenue only when you receive the payment, you are using *cash basis* accounting. One advantage of accrual basis accounting is that it helps accurately calculate earnings (or profit) from operations. This is why the private sector uses accrual basis accounting in its financial reporting. In U.S. state and local governments, the statement of net assets and the statement of activities are prepared on the accrual basis.

However, sometimes, the purpose of financial reporting in government is not to determine earnings, but rather to reflect whether sufficient financial resources are collected timely and legally to meet financial responsibilities and whether net financial resources are available for future use. This is why the *modified accrual basis* is used to prepare some fund-level financial statements in governments. According to the modified accrual basis, revenues are reported as they become available and measurable, and expenditures are reported as they become legally obligated to be paid. The following is a summary of different accounting bases for reporting revenues and expenditures.

Accounting Bases for Reporting Revenues

- The cash basis—the revenue is reported when the cash payment is received.
- The accrual basis—the revenue is reported when it is earned.
- The modified accrual basis—the revenue is recorded when it is "measurable and available." "Available" means that it must be collectible within the year or shortly after it. Sixty days or less after the end of the year is the time period widely used as a measure of availability. Note that because taxes levied during this year are expected to be collected within sixty days after the completion of the current year, they are considered to be both measurable and available. Therefore, except the portion that is not collectible within sixty days after the end of a fiscal year, taxes are considered as revenues under the modified accrual basis.

Accounting Bases for Reporting Expenses (Expenditures)

- The cash basis—an expense is recorded when cash is paid.
- The accrual basis—an expense is incurred when a resource has been used in the process of generating revenues.
- The modified accrual basis—an expense occurs when the organization becomes legally obligated to pay and that the payment will be made.

A Case Study

In the case study in Chapter 9, Joe Klein used the statement of net assets to learn the city of Evergreen's finances. In that case, Joe compiled a list of questions during the review of the statement, and one question concerned the cause of the $50,000 net asset decline. Since this decline reduced the city's financial reserve, it was one of the first concerns to be addressed. To understand what caused the decline, Joe did the following.

Step 1: Examining the Statement of Activities

Joe first reviewed the city's revenues and expenses in the statement shown in Table 10.3. In the review, he realized that public safety accounted for 63.8 percent of total net expenses of governmental activities ($1,447,000/ $2,268,000 = 63.8 percent). He also realized that the parking service, which should break even as a business-type activity, lost $60,000. On the revenue side, property taxes accounted for 57.9 percent of total general revenues ($1,250,000/$2,158,000 = 57.9 percent), which may suggest that the city overrelies on this revenue source. Overreliance on any single revenue source is dangerous, as any decline of the revenue would significantly reduce the city's total revenues.

Step 2: Comparing with Last Year's Statement

To further understand the cause of the net assets decline, Joe compared the statements of activities for the past two years. The comparison in Table 10.4 indicates that net expenses changed very little during the period. In fact, net expenses for the primary government decreased by only $2,000 ($2,210,000 − $2,208,000), although the increase in the parking net expense was a concern. On the other hand, general revenues declined by $72,000 ($2,158,000 − $2,230,000). A closer examination of this decline reveals a dramatic drop of investment earnings by $136,000 ($179,000 − $43,000). This decrease completely wiped out the revenue increases in

Table 10.4

Comparison of Net (Expenses) Revenues and General Revenues: The City of Evergreen, Florida, for the Year Ending December 31, 2004

Function/Program	Net (expenses) revenues	
	12/31/2004	12/31/2003
Governmental activities		
General government	(280,000)	(260,000)
Public safety	(1,447,000)	(1,540,000)
Transportation	(391,000)	(360,000)
Health and human services	(150,000)	(130,000)
Total	(2,268,000)	(2,290,000)
Business-type activities		
Water	30,000	20,000
Sewer	90,000	90,000
Parking	(60,000)	(30,000)
Total	60,000	80,000
Total primary government	(2,208,000)	(2,210,000)
General revenues		
Taxes		
Property taxes	1,250,000	1,240,000
Sales taxes	320,000	330,000
Franchise taxes	230,000	230,000
Grants not restricted	260,000	200,000
Investment earnings	43,000	179,000
Miscellaneous	55,000	51,000
Total general revenues	2,158,000	2,230,000
Change in net assets	(50,000)	20,000

grants not restricted ($60,000 = $260,000 – $200,000), and in property taxes ($10,000 = $1,250,000 – $1,240,000).

Step 3: Searching for Solutions and Taking Action

Joe suspected that the investment decline was the result of last year's bond market meltdown. His suspicion was confirmed by his conversation with the finance director. The finance director told him that the city's investment in a state investment pool had been largely placed in the bond market. On the basis of this analysis, Joe decided to make the following adjustments. First, he asked for a review of the city's investment policies. The review would be conducted by the finance department. The purpose of the review was to evaluate investment risks and explore potential new ways of investment. Second, he asked for a forecast of investment return for the next three years and the potential revenue shortfall as a result of decline in investment incomes. Third, he told the finance director to develop a strategy to diversify the city's revenue sources to avoid possible negative consequences of overreliance on property taxes.

Exercises

1. Key Terms

Statement of activities
Governmental activities
Business-type activities
Expenses
Indirect expenses
Direct services
Revenues
Program revenues
General revenues
Net (expenses) revenues
Special items
Transfers
Change in net assets
Accrual basis
Cash basis
Modified accrual basis

2. CAFR

Access the CAFR of a government for the last three years. Refer to the statement of activities to compare changes in expenses, program revenues, net (expenses) revenues, general revenues, and changes in net assets. Identify any changes that cause concern.

CHAPTER 11

Financial Reporting and Analysis

Fund-Level Statements

Learning Objectives

After studying this chapter, you should be able to

- Understand the use of funds in governments
- Understand key elements in fund-level statements
- Use the information in fund-level statements in financial analysis

Let us say that you are a working professional and you have two bank accounts. You use a checking account to handle daily expenses and an investment account to grow retirement income. Each time you get a check, you split the money into these two accounts. Why do you use two separate accounts? Because the separation helps you control, plan, and manage your financial life. Each account serves a different financial goal and requires different financial strategies and practices in operation. For example, the purpose of a checking account is the facilitation of daily operations, so convenience of banking is necessary. On the other hand, the investment account is designed to grow income in keeping with long-term investment strategy.

Similarly, governments have different financial operations. As discussed in previous chapters, they have operations that support governmental activities, as well as operations related to business-type activities. Governments may also play the role of trustees or guardians for certain financial resources. Financial operations of different activities have different goals and require different strategies and practices. For these and other reasons, governments' financial operations should be accounted for differently—in separate funds. This is why governments use fund accounting and reporting. Fund accounting and reporting has a unique advantage. When transactions of financial resources are accounted for in separate funds, monitoring these transactions becomes relatively easy. So the use of funds serves the ultimate purpose of financial accountability in the public sector. In this chapter, we study important concepts in funds, key components in fund-level financial statements, and how to use fund-level statements in financial analysis.

Concepts and the Tool

As introduced in Chapter 7, a fund is a fiscal and accounting entity in which financial transactions of specific types of activities are recorded and reported. Two conditions must be met to construct a fund. First, a fund is a fiscal entity in which assets are set aside for liabilities incurred in supporting specific activities of the fund. The fund reports its own assets, liabilities, and the *fund balance,* which is the difference between assets and liabilities. Second, a fund is an accounting entity in which the double-entry mechanism must be used in recording transactions. The accounting equation for a government fund can be expressed as:

$$\text{Assets} = \text{Liabilities} + \text{Fund Balance}$$

Two concepts are important in understanding a fund. One is the accounting basis discussed in previous chapters. Another is the measurement focus of a fund. *Measurement focus* refers to the subject of reporting, or, what information is expressed in reporting. Since a fund is an accounting entity, it needs to specify what information it accounts for. If the accounting and reporting of a fund focuses on net assets or incomes, its measurement focus is the *income determination* (or the *economic resources measurement*). If a fund focuses on the availability of financial resources to support its financial obligations of providing services, the measurement focus is the *current financial resource measurement.* In general, funds used in U.S. state and local governments are classified into several fund types that include *governmental funds, proprietary funds,* and *fiduciary funds.*

Governmental Funds

In previous chapters we learned that governments provide public goods, such as public safety and fire protection, as well as nonpublic goods, such as power, water, and toll roads. In general, the activities involved in providing public goods are governmental activities. The financial transactions incurred in supporting governmental activities are accounted for and reported in governmental funds. As you can imagine, because governments are mainly involved in governmental activities, governmental funds typically track the basic and major activities of a government.

Because the governmental funds account for basic activities of a government, they are concerned with financing these activities on a current basis, and they stress the availability and accountability of financial resources for occurring current financial obligations. Therefore, governmental funds use a current financial resource measurement focus, accounting for financial resources (i.e., cash and other current assets) used in providing basic government services. Governmental fund statements report current assets and current liabilities only. Noncurrent assets and liabilities, which are included in governmentwide statements such as the statement of net assets, are not reported in the governmental fund statements. The governmental funds use the modified accrual basis of accounting. Revenues are recognized when they become measurable and available. Expenses are reported when a financial obligation is incurred and the payment will be made from currently available financial resources.

The governmental funds include the general fund, special revenue funds, capital project funds, and debt service funds. The *general fund* accounts for most basic services provided by a government and most of its daily operations. These services and operations are often in areas of public safety, transportation, education, human services, parks and recreation, and general administration. Any activities not accounted for in any other funds are accounted for in the general fund. *Special revenue funds* are used to account for resources that are legally restricted for specific identifiable purposes. For example, a tax on gasoline consumption specifically restricted to highway construction and maintenance may be accounted for in a special revenue fund. Special revenue funds are different from the general fund where revenues are not specifically restricted for certain purposes. *Capital project funds* are designed to account for receipts and disbursements of resources used for financing the construction or purchase of major capital assets. In general, capital project funds should be used to account for capital projects that are financed through long-term debts or using accumulated financial resources. *Debt service funds* account for the accumulated resources to pay off principal and interest on long-term debts. The revenues of debt service funds are often in form of revenues transferred from the general fund or other funds. Expenditures in debt service funds are payments of principal and interest on long-term governmental debts.

In general, there are two financial statements for the governmental funds—the *balance sheet* and the *statement of revenues, expenditures, and changes in fund balance.* The former contains the current assets, current liabilities, and the fund balance, while the latter reports revenues, expenditures, and changes in the fund balance. In U.S. state and local governments, individual fund statements are often combined by fund types to save presentation space. Tables 11.1 and 11.2 present examples of statements for the general fund.

Table 11.1

Balance Sheet of the General Fund, December 31, 2004: The City of Evergreen ($)

Assets	
Cash	225,000
Accounts receivable	84,000
Inventory	0
Total	309,000
Liabilities	
Accounts payable	175,000
Due to other funds	70,000
Total	245,000
Fund balance	
Reserved	13,000
Unreserved	51,000
Total	64,000
Total liabilities and fund balance	309,000

Table 11.2

The Statement of Revenues, Expenditures, and Changes in Fund Balance, the General Fund, December 31, 2004: The City of Evergreen ($)

Revenues	
Property taxes	1,150,000
Sales taxes	320,000
Franchise taxes	230,000
Intergovernmental revenues	300,000
Investment earnings	38,000
Fees and fines	24,000
Total revenues	2,062,000
Expenditures	
General government	255,150
Public safety	1,317,500
Transportation	311,850
Health and human services	296,900
Total expenditures	2,181,400
Excess (deficiency) of revenues over expenditures	(119,400)
Other financing sources (uses)	
Transfer in	200,300
Transfer out	(100,000)
Total other financing sources (uses)	100,300
Net change in fund balances	(19,100)
Fund balances—beginning	83,100
Fund balances—ending	64,000

Proprietary Funds

In governments, financial transactions incurred in providing business-type goods and services are accounted for in proprietary funds, and reported as such in the financial statements. Business-type activities are often funded through user charges that are intended to cover all costs of the activities. As the purpose of most proprietary-type activities is the determination of net income, proprietary funds use the income determination measurement focus. Proprietary fund statements are prepared on the accrual basis and therefore revenues are reported when earned and expenses are reported when a resource has been consumed in the process of generating revenues.

There are two types of proprietary funds. They are *enterprise funds* and *internal service funds*. Enterprise funds are used when resources are provided primarily through the use of service charges to those receiving the benefit, or when a matching of revenues and expenses in a break-even fashion is desired. *Internal service funds* are used to account for services provided within a government by one branch to another on a cost reimbursement basis. For example, an internal service fund can be used for the financial operations of a government-operated print shop that provides printing services to other departments or units in the government. The financial statements of proprietary funds include the *statement of net assets;* the *statement of revenues, expenses, and changes in net assets;* and the *statement of cash flows*. The last statement is used to identify the sources of cash flows and how the cash is used.

Fiduciary Funds

The fiduciary funds account for resources that the government possesses in a trustee or agency capacity on behalf of individuals, other governments, or private organizations. The fiduciary funds cannot be used to support the government's own programs and operations. For example, a government can act as a trustee holding assets on behalf of employees participating in governmental pension plans. A state government can act as a trustee or agency to collect sales taxes on behalf of local governments. In general, fiduciary funds use the income determination measurement focus and the accrual basis of accounting (except for certain pension-related liabilities).

Among fiduciary funds, *pension trust funds* account for resources held in trust for employees covered under the government's retirement pension plans. *Agency funds* account for assets held temporarily by a governmental unit as the agent for individuals, organizations, other funds, or other governmental units. *Investment trust funds* account for the assets invested on behalf of other governmental organizations. *Private-purpose trust funds* are used to account for all other trust arrangements under which the principal and income are held for the benefit of individuals, other governments, and private agencies. The financial statements of fiduciary funds include the *statement of fiduciary net assets* and the *statement of changes in fiduciary net assets*.

A Case Study

In last two chapters, Joe Klein of Evergreen analyzed two governmentwide financial statements—the statement of net assets and the statement of activities. Now Joe feels that it is time to look into some specific areas of financial operations for improvement. The city has a general fund, a Community Development and Improvement Project Fund (a capital project fund), a Bond Note Redemption and Interest Fund (a debt service fund), several special revenue funds, a water/sewer system fund (an enterprise fund), and a parking system fund (an enterprise fund). Among these funds, the general fund is the largest, with 66.7 percent of total revenues (General Fund Revenues/(General Revenues + Program Revenues) = $2,062,000/($2,158,000 + $932,000)). General fund expenditures account for 69.5 percent of total expenses ($2,181,400/$3,140,000). (See Tables 10.3 and 11.2 for the source of these figures.) The general fund supports the basic services of the city, which include policing, local road/street construction and maintenance, health and human services, general administration, and other local services.

Step 1: Reviewing the Fund Statements

Joe started with the balance sheet and the statement of revenues, expenditures, and change in fund balance. To have an overview of revenues and expenditures, Joe created Table 11.3. It shows that taxes are the major revenue sources for the general fund. About 83 percent of total general fund revenues are taxes, with the property taxes representing the largest single revenue source for the general fund (55.8 percent). The table also shows that, while the city has four major functions that each account for more than 10 percent of total expenditures, the largest funded function is public safety (60.4 percent).

Step 2: Comparing with Last Year's Statements

After the overview, Joe realized that the general fund was running a deficit of $19,100 (See Net change in fund balances in Table 11.2.) The deficit seems to be caused by overspending revenue by $119,400. This fund deficit caused

Table 11.3

**The General Fund Revenues and Expenditures in 2004:
The City of Evergreen**

	Amount ($)	Percentage
Revenues		
Property taxes	1,150,000	55.8
Sales taxes	320,000	15.5
Franchise taxes	230,000	11.2
Intergovernmental revenues	300,000	14.5
Investment earnings	38,000	1.8
Fees and fines	24,000	1.2
Total revenues	2,062,000	100.0
Expenditures		
General government	255,150	11.7
Public safety	1,317,500	60.4
Transportation	311,850	14.3
Health and human services	296,900	13.6
Total expenditures	2,181,400	100.0

Joe to further examine individual revenue and expenditure items. He pulled out last year's statement and compared it with this year's. The results are shown in Table 11.4.

The comparison shows several important findings. First, although the revenue increased by $4,000 this year, the expenditure increased by $206,100. This is a 10.4 percent increase! Expenditure growth in public safety ($172,500) is the major cause of this spending increase. In fact, about 84 percent ($172,500/$206,100 = 83.7 percent) of the total expenditure increase can be contributed to the increase in public safety spending. Second, the revenue increase has slowed in comparison with the expenditure increase. The major revenue source, the property tax, has only increased by $10,000, or less than 1 percent ($10,000/$1,140,000 = 0.88 percent). Third, the major increase in revenue came from intergovernmental revenues, which had a 9.1 percent increase ($25,000/$275,000). However, this revenue source fluctuates over time and is considered an unreliable revenue source.

Step 3: Analyzing the Issues

The increase in public safety did not come as a surprise to Joe. The city has experienced a steady increase in misdemeanor cases and in traffic violations

Table 11.4

The Revenue and Expenditure Comparison: The General Fund in the City of Evergreen ($)

	2004 amount (1)	2003 amount (2)	Difference (1) − (2)
Revenues			
Property taxes	1,150,000	1,140,000	10,000
Sales taxes	320,000	330,000	(10,000)
Franchise taxes	230,000	230,000	0
Intergovernmental revenues	300,000	275,000	25,000
Investment earnings	38,000	60,000	(22,000)
Fees and fines	24,000	23,000	1,000
Total revenues	2,062,000	2,058,000	4,000
Expenditures			
General government	255,150	260,100	(4,950)
Public safety	1,317,500	1,145,000	172,500
Transportation	311,850	300,200	11,650
Health and human services	296,900	270,000	26,900
Total expenditures	2,181,400	1,975,300	206,100
Excess (deficiency) of revenues over expenditures	(119,400)	82,700	
Other financing sources (uses)			
Transfer in	200,300	150,000	
Transfer out	(100,000)	(225,000)	
Total	100,300	(75,000)	
Net change in fund balances	(19,100)	7,700	

and domestic violence. The police chief requested three additional patrol officers, the related police equipment, and supplementary spending. The chief eventually got two patrol officers. The increase in public safety appeared to be the result of this hiring.

Joe believed expenditure growth in the police department would continue while the city becomes "urbanized." The question is, how to pay for the increased service costs? Among the general fund revenue sources, property taxes have been the largest source of revenues. By analyzing the change in the property tax rate (the millage), Joe realized the millage for city services has changed little during the past decade, from 2.296 ten years ago to 2.304 now. In fact, in five of the ten years during this period, the millage declined

Table 11.5

**The Millage of Local Real Property Taxes for Citywide Services:
The City of Evergreen**

Year	Rate
2004	2.304
2003	2.352
2002	2.431
2001	2.215
2000	2.413
1999	2.259
1998	2.492
1997	2.346
1996	2.384
1995	2.296

from the previous year (see Table 11.5). This was probably the result of the city's policy of rolling back the property tax. The rollback policy was an attempt to keep the property tax amount stable when the property tax base (the assessed property values) changes. In theory, it requires the adjustment of the millage in response to the change of the assessed property valuation to achieve an equalized effect on the actual property tax amount paid by the taxpayer. More specifically, during the times of assessed value escalation, the millage is lowered, and during the times of assessed value decline, the millage is higher. However, in reality, since property values often increase, the rollback method hurts the city more than helps it. The rollback method hurts Evergreen's finances by limiting its taxation capacity. It won't allow the city to gain financially at the pace of a blooming local property market. As the property taxes are the major revenue sources for Evergreen, this rollback method limits the city's revenue flexibility and capacity significantly.

Step 4: Searching for Solutions

Joe believes that if the city does not increase the millage significantly, it will face a revenue shortage in a few years. But he is not quite sure how much the revenue shortage will be, and he doesn't know the political and legal feasibility of raising the millage. He knows that a nearby city has levied a tax on the consumption of public utilities such as water, power, phone, and cable services. Joe wants to explore the feasibility of such a new tax in his city, and decides to conduct a resource development analysis to estimate the revenue shortage, and develop possible revenue options.

Exercises

1. Key Terms

Accounting equation for funds
Fund balances
Governmental funds
Measurement focus
Income determination (economic resource measurement) focus
Current financial resource measurement focus
General fund
Special revenue funds
Capital project funds
Debt service funds
Balance sheet for funds
Statement of revenues, expenditures, and changes in fund balance
Proprietary funds
Enterprise funds
Internal service funds
Fiduciary funds
Pension trust funds
Agency funds
Investment trust funds
Private-purpose trust funds
The millage

2. CAFR

Access a state or local government's CAFR for the last two years.

1. Go to the General Fund Balance Sheet (likely included in the Governmental Funds Balance Sheet). Compare key assets, liabilities, and the fund balance for the past two years. Point out any change that causes concern.
2. Go to the Revenues, Expenditures, and Changes in Fund Balances—General Fund section (likely included in the Revenues, Expenditures, and Changes in Fund Balances—Governmental Funds section). Compare key items of revenues and expenditures and fund balance for the past two years. Specify any change that causes concern.
3. Go to the Statement of Net Assets—Proprietary Funds. Compare

key accounts of assets, liabilities, and net assets for the past two years. Specify any change that causes concern. If a jurisdiction has multiple enterprise funds, which is very likely, you could add up the items in all of the funds or select one or two of the largest funds for your analysis.

4. Go to the Revenues, Expenditures, and Changes in Net Assets—Proprietary Funds section. Compare key items of revenues, expenditures, and change in net assets for the past two years. Specify any change that causes concern. If a jurisdiction has multiple enterprise (or internal service) funds, you could add up the items in all of the funds or select one or two of the largest funds for your analysis.

5. Go to the Statement of Cash Flows—Proprietary Funds. Compare the key sources of cash flows for the past two years. Specify any change that causes concern. Again, if a jurisdiction has multiple funds in this fund category, you could add up the items in all of the funds or select one or two of the largest funds for your analysis.

6. Go to the Statement of Fiduciary Net Assets. Compare key accounts of assets, liabilities, and net assets for the past two years. Specify any change that causes concern. If a jurisdiction has multiple fiduciary funds, you could add up the items in all of the funds or select one or two of the largest funds for your analysis.

7. Go to the Statement of Changes in Fiduciary Net Assets. Compare key accounts of additions, deductions, and net assets for the past two years. Specify any change that causes concern. Again, if a jurisdiction has multiple fiduciary funds, you could add up the items in all of the funds or select one or two of the largest funds for your analysis.

CHAPTER 12

Financial Condition Analysis

Learning Objectives

After studying this chapter, you should be able to

- Know what financial condition analysis is
- Determine measures to assess financial condition
- Identify any warning trend of a deteriorating financial condition
- Specify relationships in financial condition analysis
- Explain relationships in financial condition analysis
- Write a financial condition analysis report

Why do you see a doctor? You are either sick or go for a regular physical checkup. If you are sick, the doctor often asks you a few questions about your symptoms, does some lab tests, and then prescribes medicines or recommends further treatments. In this process of diagnosis and treatment, the doctor identifies the causes of the problem and, more important, develops a strategy to improve your health.

Doing a financial condition analysis is like seeing a doctor. Heads of an organization have concerns or want to know about its health; they want to know what factors influence its health and what to do to improve it.

Concepts and the Tool

What Is Financial Condition Analysis?

Financial condition analysis (FCA) is a thorough evaluation of the financial health of an organization. Using FCA, you want to determine the financial condition of your organization, but more important, you want to determine what you can do to improve it. Therefore, *the ultimate purpose of FCA is to identify the factors that impact financial condition and to provide recommendations to improve the financial condition.*

What are the differences between FCA and the analysis of financial statements discussed in the previous three chapters? Perhaps the most salient difference is that FCA stresses the importance of socioeconomic and organizational factors in analysis, while analysis of financial statements has a narrower focus on the financial information. FCA considers socioeconomic and organizational factors the causes of financial condition.

What are the differences between FCA and the financial performance monitoring discussed in Chapter 7? Financial monitoring is conducted more frequently than FCA. Monitoring can be conducted daily or monthly on a very limited number of selected factors. FCA is a more thorough assessment process that requires more time and resources for data collection and analytical design; it may not be conducted as often as financial monitoring.

When to conduct FCA? FCA may be performed at the beginning of a fiscal period, when a budget is developed, or at the end of the period, when a financial report is prepared. It can also be conducted during a financial crisis, emergency, or distress. Finally, it can be part of an organization's strategic planning process in which financial condition is assessed to examine the organization's financial capabilities to support its mission and goals.

Who conducts FCA? FCA can be performed by an organization's internal management team, its independent auditors, or outside consultants. The internal approach has the advantage of ready accessibility to information, while outside consultants or auditors may be more objective in analysis and presenting critical recommendations.

How difficult is FCA? FCA can be rather complex. The FCA modeling process could be complicated. Measures and data may not be available. In general, the difficulty level of an FCA is determined by three factors. First, the *scope of FCA* determines analytical complexity. Financial condition has four dimensions, defined as cash solvency, budget solvency, long-run solvency, and service solvency. An analysis can focus on any single dimension or combinations of dimensions. Obviously, an FCA that examines all four dimensions of financial condition is more complex than an FCA limited to one dimension. Second, the availability of measures and data also affect the difficulty of the analysis. If measures or data are not available or not accessible, surrogates or replacements must be found and used. Third, FCA requires the specification and testing of how financial condition is affected by socioeconomic/organizational factors. The process of specification is called *FCA modeling,* which can be a rather complex process. The complexity is augmented by a lack of quality theories in the FCA literature.

Determining Measures in FCA

After the scope of the FCA is determined, necessary measures need to be developed and related data should be collected. Since the purpose of FCA is to identify socioeconomic/organizational factors that affect the financial condition, measures of financial condition and socioeconomic/organizational factors need to be developed.

Measuring Financial Condition

Financial condition is defined as the ability of an organization to meet its financial obligations. During the process of providing goods and services, an organization incurs financial obligations in the form of expenses, expenditures, or debts. All of these obligations must be paid sooner or later. If the organization can pay these obligations without incurring much financial hardship, we say that the organization's ability to pay is high and the organization is in good financial condition.

The ability to pay is commonly called *solvency* in finance. There are four levels of solvency. *Cash solvency* is the ability to generate sufficient cash to pay for current liabilities. *Budgetary solvency* refers to the ability to generate sufficient revenues to pay expenditures or expenses. The ability to pay for long-term obligations is the concept of *long-run solvency*. Finally, *service solvency* refers to the ability to pay for the existing level and quality of services now and in the future.

How to measure financial condition? A good financial condition measure should satisfy at least three criteria. First, a measure must assess a specified element of financial condition (i.e., *measurement validity*). For example, a revenue/expenditure ratio is a valid measure for budgetary solvency, which assesses the sufficiency of revenues to cover expenditures. It is not a valid measure for cash solvency, because not all revenues are in the form of cash. Second, the elements used in formulating a measure should be consistent and objective (i.e., *measurement reliability*). If the unit of a measure is the general fund (i.e., general fund revenues, general fund expenditures, the fund balance of the general fund), this unit should be used consistently. Changing the unit will lead to measurement inaccuracy and, worse, incorrect results for the FCA. Finally, the measure and supporting data should be affordable to obtain (i.e., *measurement affordability*). The cost of obtaining measures and data should always be considered in selecting measures. Everything else being equal, the less costly measure is always a better measure.

Based on these criteria, in this chapter a list of example measures is developed to assess financial condition. Effort is made to select only two measures for each dimension of financial condition. Two ratios are used to measure cash solvency. The *cash ratio* relates cash, cash equivalents, and marketable securities to current liabilities. The ratio indicates the extent of assets available to pay off current liabilities. A higher ratio indicates a better level of cash solvency.

$$Cash\ Ratio = \frac{Cash\ and\ Cash\ Equivalents + Marketable\ Securities}{Current\ Liabilities}$$

Another ratio of cash solvency is the *quick ratio*. Compared with the cash ratio, the quick ratio is a more lenient measure, because it includes noncash assets, such as receivables, as assets to pay off current liabilities. A higher ratio indicates a better level of cash solvency.

$$Quick\ Ratio = \frac{Cash\ and\ Cash\ Equivalents + Marketable\ Securities + Receivables}{Current\ Liabilities}$$

Budgetary solvency can be measured by the *operating ratio*, which assesses the sufficiency of revenues to cover expenditures. A higher value of the ratio indicates a better level of budgetary solvency.

$$Operating\ Ratio = \frac{Total\ Revenues}{Total\ Expenditures\ (Expenses)}$$

Another measure of budgetary solvency is the *own-source ratio*, which indicates the level of revenue that comes from a government's own sources, such as taxes, charges, fees, and other revenues. Since these revenues are considered more stable and controllable by the government than revenues from intergovernmental financial assistance, a higher own-source ratio indicates a higher level of budgetary solvency.

$$Own\text{-}Source\ Ratio = \frac{Revenues\ of\ Own\ Sources}{Total\ Revenues}$$

Two measures can be used for long-run solvency. The *net-asset ratio* assesses the extent of a government to withstand financial emergencies during economic slowdowns, loss of major taxpayers, and natural disasters. A higher ratio indicates a better state of long-run solvency.

$$Net\ Asset\ Ratio = \frac{Total\ Net\ Assets}{Total\ Assets}$$

Another measure of long-run solvency is the *long-term debt ratio,* which assesses an organization's ability to pay off its long-term debts. A higher ratio of this measure indicates a worse level of long-run solvency.

$$Long\text{-}Term\ Debt\ Ratio = \frac{Total\ Long\text{-}Term\ Debt}{Total\ Assets\ (or\ Total\ Revenues)}$$

Service solvency can be assessed by *net assets per capita,* which indicates the level of net assets in relation to population. A higher ratio indicates a better level of service solvency.

$$Net\ Assets\ Per\ Capita = \frac{Total\ Net\ Assets}{Population}$$

Another measure of service solvency is *long-term debt per capita,* which assesses the level of long-term debt for each resident. A higher ratio indicates that a government carries more long-term debt per capita and suggests a deteriorating state of service solvency.

$$Long\text{-}Term\ Debt\ Per\ Capita = \frac{Total\ Long\text{-}Term\ Debt}{Population}$$

Measuring Socioeconomic/Organizational Factors

There are a large number of *socioeconomic/organizational factors* that influence financial condition. Including all of them in an FCA is impossible or very costly. Selection of proper factors is critical. In addition to the above-mentioned principles of measurement validity, reliability, and affordability, two other criteria should also be considered in selecting socioeconomic/organizational factors in an FCA.

First, a theoretical cause-effect relationship must be developed to indicate how a socioeconomic/organizational factor impacts financial condition. For example, since population growth can result in more taxpayers and therefore more revenues, inclusion of population (a demographic factor) in an FCA that uses revenues in measuring financial condition is justifiable. On the other hand, the relationship between the number of school-age children in the city and revenues is rather difficult to develop, therefore the number of school-age children should not be included in the FCA. This criterion is called the *theoretical justification* of measurement. It is the most important measurement selection criterion in FCA.

The second criterion in measurement selection is that a measure is better if it is more controllable by public officials. "Controllable" means that a measure is sensitive to policies or managerial operations or other human actions of the organization. For example, a city may find that the residents' income level improves financial condition (i.e., higher-income residents are larger taxpayers). However, it is rather difficult for the city to improve residents' incomes quickly and it often takes years, therefore the city may not be able to use income growth to improve financial condition quickly. On the other hand, if a city finds that higher educational levels among city financial employees also improve its financial condition (a higher educational level suggests a higher level of professionalism), the city can relatively quickly improve its financial condition by hiring people with higher education degrees. This measurement selection criterion is called *measurement controllability*. It should be considered in order to make the result of a FCA more meaningful for decision or policy making. In general, organizational factors have higher measurement controllability than socioeconomic factors.

Table 12.1 presents a list of possible socioeconomic/organizational measures that can be used in FCA. The list is by no means an exhaustive one. It only serves as an example of possible measures in FCA. Other measures are available and should also be considered.

Identifying Any Warning Trend of Deteriorating Financial Condition

After financial condition measures are developed and related data are collected, we should examine the data to identify any possible warning trend of deteriorating financial condition. This step requires an examination of at least three periods of data for a specified financial condition measure. A three-period continuing deterioration of a measure constitutes a financial warning trend. For example, if the cash ratio for the past three years was 0.75, 0.60, and 0.55 respectively, this downward turn indicates a continuing deterioration of the measure and constitutes a financial warning trend. The Chart-Wizard function in Excel spreadsheet software is a good graphing function that provides a visual representation of a warning trend.

It is important to note that, although a warning trend provides a strong reason to conduct an FCA, it is not the only reason. The fluctuation (rather than continuation) of a financial condition measure may also deserve a close look. Sometimes, management may simply want an FCA to explore the possibilities of a continually improving financial condition or to gain insight as to the financial condition or financial capacity of the organization.

Table 12.1

Socioeconomic/Organizational Factors in FCA

Measure	Description or examples
Socioeconomic factors	
Population	The number of residents
Income	Median or mean household income, or median or mean personal income
Property values	Total assessed property values, or total taxable property values
Education level	The average number of school years completed by residents
Age	Median or mean resident age
Employment rate	Percentage of employed population to total employment-eligible population
Commercial development or business activities	The number of businesses, the value of commercial property, or the number or value of new businesses during a certain period
Organizational factors	
Budget management	Budgetary systems and practices on budget formation, implementation, and evaluation (e.g., tax rates)
Cash management	Systems and practices in managing cash (e.g., availability of mandated cash management policy)
Investment management	Systems and practices in investment (e.g., availability of periodic review of investment policies)
Fallback management	Systems and practices in upholding and using financial reserves (e.g., availability of mandated "rainy day fund")
Accounting and reporting	Accounting and reporting systems and practices (e.g., use of cost accounting)
Internal control	Systems and practices in decentralizing budgeting and procurement (e.g., availability of a decentralized procurement system)
Professionalism and leadership	Qualification or behaviors of financial personnel (e.g., mean years of education of financial personnel)

Note: This table is derived partly from the Ph.D. dissertation of Lynda M. Dennis, "Determinants of Financial Condition: A Study of U.S. Cities," University of Central Florida, 2005.

Table 12.2

Population and Revenues

Year	Population	Revenues ($)
Five years ago	173,122	198,837,119
Four years ago	176,373	265,927,499
Three years ago	180,462	249,374,988
Two years ago	184,639	265,884,544
One year ago	188,013	272,805,096

Specifying the Relationship

At the beginning of this chapter we said that the purpose of FCA is to find out the factors that *impact* financial condition. In this section, we discuss how to identify the impact. A basic principle in logic is that in order to say that Event A impacts Event B, both events must first be *related*. In other words, to prove that a factor impacts financial condition, this factor and our financial condition must be related. There is a *relationship* between the factor and financial condition. Although a relationship doesn't mean the impact actually occurs, it does serve as a necessary condition for the impact to happen. In other words, without the relationship, the impact cannot happen.

Statisticians have developed tools to assess relationships. They call these tools *measures of associations* (association is a synonym for relationship). One measure of association is the *correlation coefficient*. Let us look at an example as to how to use this statistic in FCA. Table 12.2 shows a city's population and revenues for the last five years.

To obtain the correlation coefficient for the relationship between population and revenues, we can use the following steps in the Excel spreadsheet program:

Step 1: Input the data in an Excel spreadsheet.

Step 2: Click "Data Analysis" under the "Tools" function.

Step 3: Select "Correlation" in the "Data Analysis" window.

Step 4: Select the population and revenue data in the "Input Range" (if your input range includes the variable names "population" and "revenues," then check the "Labels in the first row").

Step 5: Select an "Output Range" that does not overlap with the data.

Step 6: Hit "OK." (See Excel Screen 12.1 for the programming and the output.)

The Excel output is a correlation coefficient matrix with "population" and "revenues" being presented as both columns and rows. The correlation

Excel Screen 12.1   **Calculating Correlation Coefficients**

coefficient between them is the figure in the cross cell of "population" and "revenues." In this case, it is 0.755. What does that mean? Two pieces of information are needed in interpreting a correlation coefficient—its direction and magnitude. A positive value of a coefficient indicates that both factors move in the same direction. In other words, when the value of one factor increases, the value of the other increases too. A negative value of a coefficient indicates that the factors move in opposite directions. The magnitude of a relationship is measured on a scale from −1.000 to 1.000. A zero (0) would mean no relationship between the two factors, while 1.000 indicates a perfectly positive relationship and −1.000 a perfectly negative relationship. Table 12.3 can be used as reference in explaining the correlation coefficient value.

In our example, since the correlation coefficient is 0.755, we say that the relationship between population and revenues is a strong positive relationship, or that they are strongly positively associated. The establishment of this relationship provides evidence that population may impact revenues. Notice that the diagonal elements of the correlation matrix are 1.000. This is because a factor is perfectly positively associated with itself.

Table 12.3

Interpretation of the Correlation Coefficient

Correlation coefficient value	Interpretation
0	No relationship
Larger than 0 but smaller than 0.500	Weak positive relationship
From 0.500 to 0.699	Moderate positive relationship
From 0.700 to 0.999	Strong positive relationship
1.000	Perfect positive relationship
−1.000	Perfect negative relationship
From −0.700 to −0.999	Strong negative relationship
From −0.500 to −0.699	Moderate negative relationship
Smaller than 0 but larger than −0.500	Weak negative relationship

Now, as an exercise, you may want to input the total expenditure data in Table 2.1 on page 26 in the Excel file. Run a correlation analysis. The correlation coefficient between population and expenditures should be 0.934, and that between revenues and expenditures should be 0.884.

Explaining the Relationship

With a correlation coefficient, we can tell if a relationship exists, and if it does, how strong it is. Nevertheless, we still don't know the *exact form* of the relationship. For example, we know that population and revenues are strongly associated, but we can't tell how much revenue will be brought in if the population increases by, say, 1,000. So, after a strong relationship is identified, the next step in FCA is to further explore the exact form of the relationship. Realize that the exact form of a relationship is important for making meaningful policy or management recommendations in FCA.

Many methods can be used to identify the exact form of a relationship. One easier method is the use of per capita statistics. Let us use the data in Table 12.4 as an example.

The exact form of the relationship between population and revenues can be described as one resident on average brings in about $1,386 in revenues. If FCA indicates the government needs to have $2,000,000 in revenues to improve its financial condition to a certain degree in the next year, it will need to bring in an estimated 1,443 residents ($2,000,000/$1,386).

When per capita statistics are not available, the growth rate and percentage can also be used in specifying the exact form of a relationship. For example, if we know that a 1 percent increase in the tax rate will bring in $1,000,000 in tax revenues, and if $2,000,000 in revenues is needed to

Table 12.4

Population, Revenues, and Revenue Per Capita

Year	Population (1)	Revenues ($) (2)	Revenue per capita ($) (2)/(1)
Five years ago	173,122	198,837,119	1,149
Four years ago	176,373	265,927,499	1,508
Three years ago	180,462	249,374,988	1,382
Two years ago	184,639	265,884,544	1,440
One year ago	188,013	272,805,096	1,451
Average			1,386

improve financial condition to a certain degree, then the tax rate should be increased by 2 percent.

Notice that, in our analysis, we examined the impact of *one* socioeconomic/organizational factor on financial condition at a time. For example, in the above case, we examined the impact of population on financial condition. In reality, it is very likely that more than one factor impacts financial condition. For instance, it is possible that both population and household income affect financial condition at the same time. When two or more socioeconomic/organizational factors are considered simultaneously in FCA, this requires the use of advanced tools that are beyond the scope of this book.

FCA Report Writing

The purpose of an FCA report is to make recommendations to improve financial condition. The report should first present the rationale of the FCA, describe the existing financial condition, and discuss the process of analysis. It should present the key findings by specifying any important socioeconomic/organizational factors that influence financial condition.

It should discuss possible policy/management options that can improve financial condition. These options may be classified as those that have an immediate impact on financial condition and those that may impact financial condition in the future. If needed, the cost and benefit of each option can be examined and presented to specify the feasibility of each option.

A Case Study

The city of Lucille (population 313,611) is located in a major metropolitan area in the southeast United States. The city provides a wide range of public services to its citizens, such as policing, fire protection, parks and recreation, city road/street construction and maintenance, library services, and many other municipal services. Lucille is located within the boundaries of Osorio County. The county provides services in the areas of correction, court services, property assessment, county road/street construction and maintenance, and many other county-level services.

In a recent management meeting, City Manager Wendy Higgins told Finance Director Jeff Bolling that a recent issue of *PA Times* published the results of a survey that indicated that about 67 percent of U.S. cities had experienced difficulty in collecting sufficient revenues to pay for their services. In other words, three out of five cities said they had a budget solvency problem. Wendy wants to know where Lucille stands in budget solvency. Wendy knows that the city's Finance Department conducts an annual FCA. But, the analysis has always focused on cash solvency—whether the city has enough cash to meet its short-term financial obligations. Jeff explained that budget solvency is different from cash solvency in that it reflects different aspects of financial condition. Wendy then asked Jeff to prepare an FCA on the budget solvency of the city that focuses on two specific questions: What is the city's current budget solvency status? And what can be done to improve budget solvency, if needed? She wanted to see the analysis in a week so she could present it to the city commission in a budget workshop.

Step 1: Defining the Scope of the Analysis

Jeff knew the scope of the analysis would be limited by several factors and he discussed these factors with Wendy to ensure that she understood these limitations. First, the analysis would focus on budget solvency only. There would be no attempt to address issues of long-term solvency and service solvency, which could be done later if needed. Also, there would be no need to repeat the analysis on cash solvency, which is always conducted at the end of a fiscal year. The main results of last year's cash solvency analysis can be seen in the CAFR. Second, the analysis would focus on governmental funds only. No attempts would be made to address the issues in other funds. This is because the data of governmental funds are readily available, and the majority of the city's expenditures are for governmental activities. The city's governmental-activity expenditures are 67 percent of the total primary government expenses.

Third, the analysis would be limited by available measures and data. As the analysis is needed in a short time, only measures and data available in the CAFR would be used. There will be no time and budget to collect data beyond the city's possession, which may be needed in a more comprehensive analysis in the future. Fourth, the analysis would be guided by the financial condition literature and experiences of city financial personnel. The latter is particularly important, as the current literature is often not specific enough for the financial environment faced by the city. Last, any recommendation made in the analysis would be valid for a time frame of no more than three years. Anyone who attempts to use the recommendations longer than that should repeat the analysis with the latest data.

Step 2: Determining Measures and Collecting Data

Jeff decided to use two indicators to measure budget solvency. The first was the operating ratio (Total Revenues/Total Expenditures), which assesses the extent of revenues to cover expenses. The revenues include program revenues and general revenues. A higher ratio indicates a higher budget solvency. More specifically, a ratio of 1.000 indicates all revenues are used to cover all expenditures. A ratio greater than 1.000 indicates revenues exceed expenditures, and a ratio less than 1.000 suggests a deficit of revenues over expenditures.

The second was the own-source ratio (Revenues from Own Sources/Total Revenues), which measures the proportion of total revenues that comes from the city's own revenue sources. A higher ratio indicates less reliance on vulnerable intergovernmental revenues and a higher level of budget solvency.

Jeff also collected information about the following socioeconomic/organizational factors that could influence budget solvency. (1) Assessed property values can affect budget solvency by affecting the property tax revenues—one of the largest revenues of the city. Assessed value increases should lead to an increase in tax revenues, and therefore improve the operating ratio and the own-source ratio. (2) Population fluctuation may influence both revenues and expenditures, and thus budget solvency. Population increase can provide more revenues through increased taxes and fees; population increase may also lead to increased spending to support more public services. (3) Income per capita in the city may also affect budget solvency. Increases in income may suggest an increase in the tax base that results in improved budget solvency. But, such increases may also suggest an increased demand for a high quality of public services, which leads to higher spending and potentially deteriorating budget solvency. (4) A higher unemployment rate may suggest a bigger need for public assistances and services, which could negatively affect budget solvency. (5) As far as the property tax rate, the millage can influence the amount of revenue collected. Given the size of assessed property values, a higher millage produces a larger amount of property taxes and a higher level of budget solvency. Jeff collected the data for expenditures, revenues, and all five socioeconomic/organizational factors for the last ten years from the city's CAFR, as shown in Table 12.5.

Table 12.5

CAFR Data for the City of Lucille

Year	Expenditures ($)	Revenues ($)	Own-source revenues ($)	Assessed property values ($)	Population	Income per capita ($)	Unemployment rate	The millage
1	157,849,000	177,879,000	153,481,000	9,448,376,000	280,699	20,156	0.064	9.384
2	166,754,000	185,672,000	159,381,000	9,544,867,000	280,587	21,193	0.052	9.397
3	171,030,000	194,113,000	165,786,000	9,727,654,000	286,320	22,624	0.044	9.342
4	182,867,000	199,831,000	169,593,000	9,923,234,000	289,790	23,914	0.038	9.304
5	188,981,000	211,625,000	179,369,000	10,700,406,000	290,920	25,277	0.033	9.144
6	201,735,000	224,660,000	192,115,000	11,734,986,000	293,920	26,355	0.028	9.056
7	211,261,000	243,258,000	209,501,000	12,842,257,000	296,720	27,304	0.026	8.931
8	223,353,000	256,644,000	223,012,000	13,841,329,000	303,447	27,458	0.026	8.816
9	234,769,000	270,847,000	236,197,000	15,744,435,000	309,104	28,784	0.036	8.691
10 (this year)	263,139,000	285,705,000	249,941,000	16,748,134,000	313,611	30,099	0.044	8.734

Table 12.6

Operating Ratio and Own-Source Revenue Ratio

Year	Operating ratio	Own-source revenue ratio
1	1.127	0.863
2	1.113	0.858
3	1.135	0.854
4	1.093	0.849
5	1.120	0.848
6	1.114	0.855
7	1.152	0.861
8	1.149	0.869
9	1.154	0.872
10	1.086	0.875
(this year)		

Step 3: Identifying Warning Trends

How is the city's budget solvency? Is there a warning trend in budget solvency? To answer these questions, Jeff used the data in the above table to compile data for the operating ratio and the own-source ratio for the past ten years, as shown in Table 12.6. Notice that the operating ratio for this year is 1.086, which is the ratio of this year's revenues ($285,705,000) to expenditures ($263,139,000). This year's own-source ratio, 0.875, is calculated from this year's own-source revenues ($249,941,000) divided by total revenues ($285,705,000).

The operating ratio shows the city had sufficient revenues to pay its bills for the past ten years. Jeff used the value of the ratio 1.000 (Revenues = Expenditures) as the benchmark to evaluate and explain the operating ratio. The ratio has been greater than the benchmark, which indicates a satisfying status of budget solvency in that indicator. The own-source ratio shows that more than 85 percent of the city's revenues came from its own sources, higher than the national average of about 70 percent for local governments. This measure shows that the city does not appear to overrely on intergovernmental revenues. As intergovernmental revenues can fluctuate over time and are not considered a reliable source of revenues, absence of overreliance on intergovernmental revenues suggests a satisfying status of budget solvency for the city.

Nevertheless, two issues concern Jeff. First, the operating ratio has fluctuated over the last five years. This year's ratio (1.086) is particularly low in comparison with those of previous years (the average of the past ten years is 1.124). Thus, there may be a need to stabilize the ratio. Second, although the own-source ratio is higher than the national average for local governments, it is still lower than that of cities with populations greater than 100,000 in the

Table 12.7

What May Affect the Operating Ratio?

	Correlation with operating ratio
Assessed property values	0.114
Population	0.072
Income per capita	0.086
Unemployment rate	−0.307
The millage rate	−0.266

Note: The figures are correlation coefficients.

state. It is also lower than several adjacent cities that have socioeconomic characteristics that are similar to Lucille's. These concerns indicate there is still room for improvement in the city's budget solvency. Jeff then decided to continue the analysis to explore possible ways to improve the budget solvency of the city.

Step 4: Specifying the Relationships

In this step, Jeff wanted to specify the impact of socioeconomic/organizational factors on budget solvency. The socioeconomic/organizational factors include assessed property values, population, income per capita, the unemployment rate, and the millage. Among them, the millage is considered an organizational factor, as it can be determined by the city's policymakers. All of the other factors are considered socioeconomic factors.

The Operating Ratio

Using the data in Table 12.5, Jeff first ran a correlation analysis of socioeconomic/organizational factors with the operating ratio. Table 12.7 shows the result.

According to our rule of thumb to judge the relationship, none of these relationships is strong (i.e., greater than 70 percent or less than −70 percent). None of these factors appear to influence the ratio directly. However, since the operating ratio is the division of revenues by expenditures (i.e., Revenues/Expenditures), one way to improve the ratio is to increase revenues. So Jeff decided to examine factors that could influence revenues. Table 12.8 shows the correlation between revenues and the socioeconomic/organizational factors.

The results show that revenues are strongly and positively associated with

Table 12.8

What May Affect Revenues?

	Correlation with revenues
Assessed property values	**0.986**
Population	**0.988**
Income per capita	**0.971**
Unemployment rate	−0.537
The millage	**−0.985**

Note: The figures are correlation coefficients. Strong relationships are highlighted in bold.

Table 12.9

What May Affect the Own-Source Ratio?

	Correlation with the own-source ratio
Assessed property values	**0.812**
Population	**0.704**
Income per capita	0.551
Unemployment rate	0.063
The millage rate	**−0.721**

Note: The figures are correlation coefficients. Strong relationships are highlighted in bold.

assessed property values, population, and income levels, which suggests that an increase in these factors leads to the increase in revenues and, therefore, the improvement of the operating ratio. The result also shows that the millage is strongly and negatively associated with revenues. Revenue increase is associated with millage decline. This bewildering relationship is the subject of a later discussion in this chapter.

The Own-Source Ratio

Jeff then ran a correlation analysis to assess the possible influences of socioeconomic/organizational factors on the own-source ratio. Table 12.9 presents the results.

The result shows that the own-source ratio is strongly and positively associated with assessed property values and population. Increase in assessed property values and population could lead to improvement of the own-source ratio. The millage is strongly and negatively associated with the ratio. Increase in the millage is associated with decline of the own-source ratio.

Figure 12.1 **The Impact of Assessed Values on Budget Solvency**

leads to   leads to

Assessed Value Increase → Revenue Increase → Improved Budget Solvency

In sum, the findings indicate that 1) increase in assessed property values and population may result in the improvement of the city's budget solvency through increase in revenues, 2) increase in income may also lead to improvement of its budget solvency through the improvement of the operating ratio, 3) nevertheless, the increase in the millage is associated with a decline in budget solvency. A further explanation of this relationship is needed.

Step 5: Explaining the Relationships

In order to make recommendations, Jeff wants to further explain the relationships between budget solvency and assessed property values, population, income, and the millage. He wants to know exactly how much these factors impact budget solvency (i.e., the exact form of these relationships).

Assessed Property Values

First, the relationship between assessed property values and budget solvency can be simply specified in Figure 12.1.

In the current year, the city has assessed property values of $16,748,134,000 and collected $285,705,000 in tax revenues. In other words, the city collected $0.0171 in revenue for every dollar of assessed value (i.e., $285,705,000/ $16,748,134,000 = 0.0171). This revenues/assessed value ratio has been consistent for the past two years. The city has experienced a real estate boom recently. It is expected that assessed property values will continue to grow at an annual rate of about $700,000,000 in the next year. This would bring the city an additional $11,970,000 ($700,000,000 × 0.0171) in revenue. As an example to illustrate exactly how assessed value affects budget solvency, this revenue increase would improve the operating ratio of the year by 0.046 (i.e., Additional Revenues/Expenditures = $11,970,000/$263,139,000 = 0.046). Notice that this is the impact of increased assessed property values without considering other factors that also influence budget solvency.

Population

Population growth can affect budget solvency in two simultaneous ways. Population growth increases the city's revenues because people pay taxes, fees, charges, and other revenues. On the other hand, population growth

Figure 12.2 **The Impact of Population on Budget Solvency**

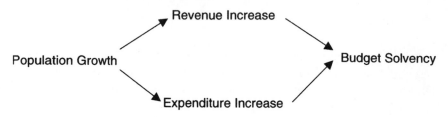

creates additional demand for city services, which increases expenditures. The impact of population on budget solvency can be simply specified in Figure 12.2.

Using the data for this year, Jeff calculated that the revenues from each resident (revenues per capita) were $911.02 ($285,705,000/313,611) and the expenditures for each resident (expenditures per capita) were $839.06 ($263,139,000/313,611). The difference is $71.96 in net revenue. The positive figure indicates that the city may gain net revenue by bringing in more people. In other words, population growth may bring more revenues than expenditures to the city. How much does the net revenue affect budget solvency? Jeff predicts a population growth of 3,500 in the next year, which will generate $251,860 ($71.96 × 3,500) in additional net revenue. In this example, the revenue increase would improve the operating ratio for the current year by 0.000957 ($251,843/$263,139,000). Jeff notes that this is only the impact of increased population without considering other factors that also influence budget solvency.

Personal Income

Personal income affects budget solvency in several ways. Income increases can prompt more personal consumption of fee- or charge-based city services and products. Therefore, personal income growth increases the city's revenues in fees or charges. Also likely is that the increase in personal income leads to increased real estate consumption (i.e., upgrade of homes, purchase of new homes or more expensive homes, purchase of lands, etc.). The correlation coefficient between income and assessed property value is 0.930. So the increase in personal income may be reflected in the increase in assessed property values. Because of this, the impact of increased personal income on budget solvency is already reflected in the impact of assessed property values on budget solvency. Thus Jeff decided not to further demonstrate this impact in his analysis in order to avoid confusion or possibility of overestimation.

Figure 12.3 **The Impact of the Millage on Budget Solvency**

The Millage

Finally, the millage appears to affect budget solvency negatively. Decrease in the millage is associated with increases in revenues and an improved own-source ratio. The negative relationship between the millage and revenues is caused by a city policy called "property tax rollback" in which the millage is adjusted for assessment of property values. According to this policy, if a significant increase in assessed property values occurs, the millage will be lowered to reduce the taxpayers' burden, which results in a direct negative relationship between assessed property values and the millage (the correlation coefficient is −0.970 for the past ten years). This negative relationship explains the negative relationship between the millage and the city's revenues and the own-source ratio. More specifically, during the past ten years, when the assessed property values increased, the millage often declined. Figure 12.3 demonstrates the impact of the millage on budget solvency.

Exactly how much of the millage change is associated with budget solvency? During the past ten years, revenues had an annual 5.42 percent increase in the city, while the millage had a 0.80 percent annual decline. If the same percentage of millage decline is expected for the next year, the revenue increase will be $15,485,211 ($285,705,000 × 5.42 percent). Then, the operating ratio will improve by 0.0589 ($15,485,211/$263,139,000). Again, this relationship is established without considering other factors that also influence revenues.

Step 6: Taking Action to Improve Financial Condition

A week later in a staff meeting, Jeff summarized the findings and recommended actions to improve budget solvency. He recommended that the operating ratio should be stabilized at an average of 1.100 for the next five years. This ratio ensures that revenues are sufficient to fund the existing level of services and the continual accumulation of the city's financial reserve. He also recommended an increase in the own-source ratio from the current 0.875 to 0.900 for the next five years in order to withstand the impact of any possible decline in intergovernmental assistance.

Jeff recommended several strategies to achieve these budget solvency goals. First, the city should continue its efforts to provide a family-friendly environment in order to attract more working people. Second, the city should maintain a quality of life environment that ensures the healthy development of the local economy and real estate market. Third, the city should stress its existing economic development strategies that attract employers that can bring high-paid jobs to the community. Fourth, the rollback policy related to the property tax rate significantly limits the city's capacity to increase revenues. A review of this policy may be necessary. Jeff argued that any significant increase in assessed property values would be offset by the rollback policy. The impact of the policy would be particularly salient during economic downturns, when the city's economy-sensitive revenue bases would be in decline. As assessed property values are less sensitive to cyclical changes in the economy, property tax revenues might be one of a few revenue options the city has to use to survive bad economic times. Any measure that eases the rollback policy to give the city flexibility in property tax rates, assessment, and collection should be considered.

Exercises

1. Key Terms

Financial condition analysis (FCA)
Purpose of FCA
Scope of FCA
FCA modeling
Financial condition
Solvency
Cash solvency
Budgetary solvency
Long-run solvency
Service solvency
Measurement validity
Measurement reliability
Measurement affordability
Cash ratio

Table 12.10

Expenditure Data (in thousands of dollars)

Year	Public safety	General government	Total
1	94,367	11,222	157,849
2	100,034	9,831	166,754
3	105,669	10,910	171,030
4	112,433	11,001	182,867
5	117,023	10,234	188,981

Quick ratio
Operating ratio
Own-source ratio
Net asset ratio
Long-term debt ratio
Net assets per capita
Long-term debt per capita
Socioeconomic/organizational factors
Theoretical justification of measurement
Measurement controllability
Warning trends
Correlation coefficient
Interpretation of correlation coefficient values
Exact form of relationship

2. Calculation

Table 12.10 shows expenditure data for the past five years in an urban city.

1. Compute the correlation coefficients for these factors.
2. Prepare a paragraph interpreting the results.

3. Application

In the case study, we examined the budgetary solvency in the city of Lucille. Now the city manager wants an analysis of all four dimensions of FCA— cash solvency, budgetary solvency, long-run solvency, and service solvency. Only data from the past five years are available for analysis. Table 12.11 presents additional data from the city's CAFR.

Table 12.11

City of Lucille's Additional Financial Data for the Past Five Years ($)

Year	Cash	Cash equivalents	Marketable securities	Receivables	Current liabilities	Net assets	Total assets
1	960,000	96,263,000	105,915,000	25,472,000	59,409,000	981,077,865	2,279,434,717
2	565,000	129,429,000	91,403,000	31,899,000	58,956,000	1,059,432,173	2,322,398,266
3	2,517,000	151,978,000	67,676,000	0	52,258,000	1,144,044,291	2,366,171,605
4	465,000	150,846,000	31,427,000	0	72,594,000	1,235,414,000	2,410,770,000
5 (this year)	777,000	209,026,000	54,316,000	3,005,000	73,549,000	1,334,081,000	2,456,209,000

Conduct an FCA to examine the cash solvency, budgetary solvency, long-run solvency, and service solvency of Lucille.

4. Application

Using any CAFR that you select, conduct an FCA.

Appendix

Exercise Answers

Chapter 1. Revenue Forecasting

2. Calculations

1. Forecast for Year 6 = (15 + 13 + 16)/3 = 14.67.
2. Using the average of the data of the first four years, we have (10 + 12 + 15 + 13)/4 = 12.50. Forecast for Year 6 = (0.8 × 16.00) + (0.2 × 12.50) = 12.80 + 2.50 = 15.30. The result from Excel should be 15.45.
3. The average of the last three increments is [3 + (–2) + 3]/3 = 1.33. Forecast for Year 6 = 16.00 + 1.33 = 17.33.

3. Calculations

1. Total revenue = 568,790 × $10.50 = $5,972,295.
2. Forecast for Year 10 = 10.40 + 5.50(10) = 65.4. Forecast for Year 11 = 10.40 + 5.50(11) = 70.9. Forecast revenue difference between Year 10 and Year 11 = 70.90 – 65.40 = 5.50. Note that this is b (or revenue increment) in the regression model.
3. APE (for the first forecast) = | 35.00 – 40.00 |/40.00 = 0.125, or 12.5 percent. APE (for the second forecast) = | 46.00 – 42.00 |/42.00 = 0.0952, or 9.52 percent. MAPE = (12.5 percent + 9.5 percent)/2 = 11.0 percent.

4. Forecasting Licenses, Permits, and Fees in the city of Sun Lake, California

1. Forecast with SMA = $18,749,757. Forecast with EXS (α = 0.8) = $19,847,140. Forecast with TMA = $20,289,136 + ($1,990,388 + $591,938 + $2,013,099)/3 = $21,820,944.

173

2. APE 1 (forecast for Year 8): SMA = $|\$18{,}749{,}757 - \$23{,}210{,}218|$ / $\$23{,}210{,}218 = 19.2$ percent. EXS = $|\$19{,}827{,}140 - \$23{,}210{,}218|$ / $\$23{,}210{,}218 = 14.5$ percent. TMA = $|\$21{,}820{,}944 - \$23{,}210{,}218$ $/\$23{,}210{,}218 = 6.0$ percent. APE 2 (forecast for Year 7): SMA = $|\$17{,}217{,}949 - \$20{,}289{,}136|/\$20{,}289{,}136 = 15.1$ percent. EXS = $|\$18{,}079{,}157 - \$20{,}289{,}136|/\$20{,}289{,}136 = 10.9$ percent. TMA = $|\$18{,}957{,}127 - \$20{,}289{,}136|/\$20{,}289{,}136 = 6.6$ percent. MAPE for: SMA = (19.2 percent + 15.1 percent)/2 = 17.2 percent, EXS = (14.5 percent + 10.9 percent)/2 = 12.7 percent, TMA = (6.0 percent + 6.6 percent)/2 = 6.3 percent. So, TMA is the most accurate method.

3. Forecast for Year 9 = $23,210,218 + [(($23,210,218 − $20,289,136) + ($20,289,136 − $18,276,037) + ($18,276,037 − $17,684,099)]/3 = $23,210,218 + ($2,921,082 + $2,013,099 + $591,938)/3 = $23,210,218 + $1,842,040 = $25,052,257. Similarly, forecast for Year 10 = $25,052,257 + $2,258,740 = $27,310,997. Forecast for Year 11 = $27,310,997 + $2,340,620 = $29,651,617. Realize that the increment increases from $1,842,040 to $2,340,620, which may not be accurate. So, a simple remedy is to use $1,842,040 for all three forecasts, which yields: forecast for Year 9 = $23,210,218 + $1,842,040 = $25,052,257, forecast for Year 10 = $25,052,257 + $1,842,040 = $26,894,297, forecast for Year 11 = $26,894,297 + $1,842,040 = $28,736,337.

4. Using Excel, forecast = $12,469,511 + $1,034,895(Year). Forecast for Year 8 = $12,469,511 + $1,034,895(8) = $20,748,671. APE 1 for regression = $|\$20{,}748{,}671 - \$23{,}210{,}218|/\$23{,}210{,}218 = 10.6$ percent. You can also compute MAPE for the regression. To do that, you need to formulate a regression equation by using data for the first six years to forecast the revenue in Year 7, which is forecast = $12,776,367 + $919,823(Year). So, the forecast for Year 7 = $12,776,367 + $919,823(7) = $19,215,128. APE 2 for regression = $|\$19{,}215{,}128 - \$20{,}289{,}136|/\$20{,}289{,}136 = 5.3$ percent. MAPE = (10.6 percent + 5.3 percent)/2 = 8.0 percent. Regression is more accurate than SMA and EXS, but less accurate than TMA.

5. Forecasting Franchise Tax in Sunbelt

First, let us forecast revenues for Year 10 and Year 11. Since this is trend data, TMA is a proper tool. Using TMA, we have: forecast for Year 10 = $17,655,000 + [($15,257,000 − $15,089,000) + ($16,749,000 − $15,257,000) + ($17,655,000 − $16,749,000)]/3 = $17,655,000 + ($168,000 + $1,492,000 + $906,000)/3 = $17,655,000 + $855,333 = $18,510,333. Forecast for Year 11 = $18,510,333 + $855,333 = $19,365,666.

Now, let us forecast the revenue for Year 12, temporarily assuming that there is no 10 percent contract increase of revenue from BellSouth. Forecast for Year 12 = $19,365,666 + $855, 333 = $20,220,999.

Let us also forecast the revenue from BellSouth with an assumption that there is no 10 percent contract increase. Using TMA, we have: forecast for Year 10 from BellSouth = $7,062,000 + [($7,062,000–$6,700,000) + ($6,700,000–$5,950,000) + ($5,950,000–$6,036,000)]/3 = $7,062,000 + $342,000 = $7,404,000. Forecast for Year 11 from BellSouth = $7,404,000 + $342,000 = $7,746,000. Forecast for Year 12 from BellSouth = $7,746,000 + $342,000 = $8,088,000

Now, a 10 percent contract increase of the revenue from BellSouth for Year 12 will bring an additional 10 percent × $8,088,000 = $808,800, which should be added to the forecast for Year 12. So, the forecast for Year 12 (with the 10 percent BellSouth contract increase) = $20,220,999 + $808,800 = $21,029,799.

6. Forecasting Miscellaneous Revenue

Since the city reclassified this revenue in Year 5, we should use data after that time. A quick review of the data from Year 6 to Year 10 does not indicate a clear trend, with two years of increase (Years 7 and 9) and two years of decline (Years 8 and 10). An application of SMA on the latest three years' data yields a forecast of $8,863,085 (($8,249,782 + $10,783,255 + $7,556,219)/3). Your response to the finance director might go something like this:

"I have decided to use this figure as a forecast basis, and take it to the financial officials of the city for their input on any significant socioeconomic or organizational changes in the city that could influence this revenue. I will make adjustment for the forecast based on these inputs. With regard to the 95 percent underestimation, it is the finance director' right to take whatever percentage he or she wants. But, it is my obligation as a forecasting professional to give the most accurate figure I can come up with."

Chapter 2. Resource Development Analysis

2. Calculation

1. Revenue this year = ($23,902,346 − $12,345,670) × 0.075 = $866,751. Revenue next year = ($24,567,390 − $16,345,670) × 0.075 = $616,629. Estimated revenue shortage = $866,751 − $616,629 = $250,122.

2. Estimation error = ($250,122 − $345,291)/$345,291 = −27.56 percent.
3. Revenue this year = ($23,902,346 − $12,345,670) × 0.075 = $866,751. Revenue next year = ($24,567,390 − $16,345,670) × 0.080 = $657,738. Estimated revenue shortage = $866,751 − $657,738 = $209,013.
4. Estimation error = ($209,013 − $345,291)/$345,291 = −39.47 percent.

3. Calculation

1. Revenue this year = ($243,578,500 × 7.08/1,000) + ($124,760,340 × 9.54/1,000) = $2,914,749.
2. Revenue next year = ($231,349,400 × 7.08/1,000) + ($100,760,350 × 9.54/1,000) = $2,599,207. So, the revenue shortage = $2,914,749 − $2,599,207 = $315,542.
3. Estimation error = ($315,542 − $275,654)/$275,654 = 14.47 percent.

4. Calculation

You need to first calculate the police expenditure per capita for the past ten years, then use these figures to compute police expenditure per capita growth rate (use the example in Table 2.1 for reference). You should arrive at an average growth rate of 4.0 percent. Last year's police expenditure per capita was $356.20 ($211,635,000/594,176). The estimated police expenditure per capita for the next year is $356.20(1.040) = $370.40.

Chapter 3. Cost Estimation

2. Calculations

1. Overhead rate = $53,340/(175 + 134) = $172.62 per student. Cost allocation to the MPA program = $172.62 × 175 students = $30,208.74.
2. Overhead rate = $124,200/1,920 = $64.69 per hour. Cost allocation to the economic development program = $64.69 × 200 hours = $12,937.50.
3. Annual network cost = ($12,000 − $2,000)/3 = $3,333.33.
4. The total of network working hours is 6,570 (2,920 + 2,190 + 1,460), and the total of work hours in the first year is 2,920. The network cost in the first year = ($12,000 − $2,000)/6,570 × 2,920 = $4,444.44.

3. Determining Cost Base

Here are examples of three administrative or office cost items and the related measures. You can come up with your own. The first cost item is a manager's salary and benefit. The measure of time spent is "the number of hours spent by the manager." The measure of output is "the number of reports produced by the manager" or "the number of directives issued by the manager." The second cost item is the electricity bill. The measure of time spent is "the number of work hours." The measure of output is "the number of products or services provided by an agency." The third cost item is office expenses. The measure of manpower used is "the number of workers." The measure of output is "the number of products produced by an agency."

4. Cost of Operations

The following information was obtained from a city's CAFR.

1. In the last year, the three most expensive functions were police, wastewater, and fire.
2. In the last year, police expenses were $82,247,630 (20.2 percent of total). Wastewater expenses were $60,340,070 (14.8 percent of total). Fire protection expenses were $46,395,168 (11.4 percent of total). The total expenses were $407,204,348.
3. Two years ago, police expenses were $73,354,220 (20.1 percent). Wastewater expenses were $60,673,007 (16.7 percent). Fire protection expenses were $36,513,281 (10.0 percent). The total expenses were $364,196,770.
4. There was an increase in total expenses by $43,007,578 ($407,204,348 − $364,196,770) during this period. This was an 11.8 percent ($43,007,578/$364,196,770) increase, which means that city services were 11.8 percent more expensive. The police expenses increased by $8,893,410 ($82,247,630 − $73,354,220). The fire expenses grew by $9,881,887. The wastewater expenses declined by $332,937. Of the total increase of $43,007,578, 20.0 percent ($8,893,410/$43,007,578) was attributed to the increase in the police expenses, and 23 percent ($9,881,887/$43,007,578) was due to the increase in the fire expenses.
5. The expenses per capita were $2,089 last year and $1,895 two years ago. The increase was $194, 10.3 percent. This suggests that the city's residents may eventually have to pay more for city services.

Chapter 4. Cost Comparison

2. Calculations

1. PV = $1,000/(1 + 0.05) = $952.38.
2. PV = $1,000/(1 + 0.05)^2 = $907.03.
3. PV = $200 + $500/(1 + 10 percent) + $500/(1 + 10 percent)^2 + $500/ (1 + 10 percent)^3 = $200.00 + $454.55 + $413.22 + $375.66 = $1,443.43. (Your Excel calculation should confirm this result.)
4. You need to solve for C in the following equation: $12,000 = C/(1 + 5 percent) + C/(1 + 5 percent)^2 + C/(1 + 5 percent)^3 + C/(1 + 5 percent)^4 + C/(1 + 5 percent)^5$, and $C = $2,771.70. You should use Excel to solve this question.
5. The question actually asks how much you have to pay monthly for the next ten years to make up $100,000 in today's value (PV). You should use Excel to solve for C in the following equation: $100,000 = C/(1 + 7 percent/12) + C/(1 + 7 percent/12)^2 + C/(1 + 7 percent/12)^3 + \ldots C/(1 + 7 percent/12)^{119} + C/(1 + 7 percent/12)^{120}$. Refer to the example of annualized cost in the text for the calculation process and Excel programming. In Excel's paste function (fx), choose the "PMT" (payment) function, and make sure to convert the annual interest rate (7 percent) to a monthly rate by dividing it by twelve. $C = $1,161.06.
6. You need to solve for C in the following equation: $100,000 = C/(1 + 7 percent/12) + C/(1 + 7 percent/12)^2 + C/(1 + 7 percent/12)^3 + \ldots C/(1 + 7 percent/12)^{239} + C/(1 + 7 percent/12)^{240}$. With the use of Excel, you should get $C = $775.27.

3. Present Value Analysis

1. When the discount rate is 5 percent, the PVC for EOP is $1,854,595, and the PVC for PMS is $1,813,785. So, PMS is less costly and should be recommended for purchase.
2. When the discount rate is 10 percent, the PVC for EOP is $1,816,987, and the PVC for PMS is $1,700,960. Again, PMS is less costly and should be recommended for purchase.
3. When the discount rate is 5 percent, the annualized cost of each option is: EOP (for six years' use) = $365,388, and PMS (for five years' use) = $418,939. So, EOP is less costly and should be recommended for purchase. This conclusion is based on the assumption that there is no cost for EOP in the sixth year, and that there is no salvage value for both systems after their lifetimes.

4. Present Value Analysis: Lease or Buy Decisions

The PVC for the buy option is $20,673. The PVC for the lease option is $19,243. So, the printer should be leased. The same conclusion should be reached with the annualized cost analysis.

Chapter 5. Incremental Cost Analysis

2. Calculations

1. TC (quantity = 15,000) = $3.0 million + $1.5 million = $4.5 million. FC (quantity = 20,000) = $3.0 million. VC (quantity = 20,000) = ($1.5 million/15,000) × 20,000 = $2.0 million. TC (quantity = 20,000) = $3.0 million + $2.0 million = $5.0 million. IC (quantity = 20,000) = $5.0 million − $4.5 million = $500,000. MC (quantity = 20,000) = $500,000/(20,000 − 15,000) = $100.
2. Similarly, FC (quantity = 30,000) = $4.5 million. VC (quantity = 30,000) = $3.0 million. TC (quantity = 30,000) = $7.5 million. IC (quantity = 30,000) = $7.5 million − $5.0 million = $2.5 million. MC (quantity = 30,000) = $250.

3. Incremental Cost Analysis

FC (quantity = 46,280) = $1,500,000 personnel cost + $15,000 office expenses + $150,000 miscellaneous + $50,000 vehicle maintenance = $1,715,000. VC (quantity = 46,280) = $69,000 gasoline + $189,000 overhead = $258,000. TC (quantity = 46,280) = $1,715,000 + $258,000 = $1,973,000. VC (quantity = 49,780) = $258,000/46,280 × 49,780 = $277,512. TC (quantity = 49,780) = $1,715,000 + $277,512 = $1,992,512. IC = $1,992,512 − $1,973,000 = $19,512. MC = $19,512/3,500 = $5.57. Because the city is willing to pay $6 per ton, higher than $5.57, the county should accept the offer. The $6 is called "marginal revenue" in economics. If marginal revenue is larger than marginal cost, there is profit.

4. Incremental Cost Analysis

The recyclable materials increase from 3,500 to 5,000 tons. That is a 1,500-ton increase. The total quantity for the second year is 49,780 + 1,500 = 51,280. Because the purchase price of the vehicle is $30,000 and the maintenance cost is $10,000 per year, FC (quantity = 51,280) = $1,715,000 + $30,000 +

$10,000 = $1,755,000. VC (quantity = 51,280) = $258,000/46,280 × 51,280 = $285,874. TC (quantity = 51,280) = $1,755,000 + $285,874 = $2,040,874. IC = $2,040,874 − $1,992,512 = $48,362. MC = $48,362/1,500 = $32.24. Because the county's marginal cost, $32.24, is larger than what the city is willing to pay, $6.00, the county should reject the city's demand for the additional service unless the city is willing to pay a fee equal to or higher than the marginal cost.

5. Incremental Cost Analysis and Zero-Based Budgeting

It would be surprising if you were to find any use of incremental costing in ZBB. This is precisely one of several reasons that ZBB fails. Many governments simply do not have capable individuals or the technical capacities required to warrant the success of ZBB.

Chapter 6. Cost-Benefit Analysis

2. Calculations

1. When the discount rate is 5 percent, the NPV for Project A = $158,650, and the NPV for Project B = $522,639.
2. When the discount rate is 10 percent, the NPV for Project A = −$73,454, and the NPV for Project B = $271,219.
3. The above analysis shows that, at the 5 percent discount rate level, both projects are economically feasible. However, Project B has higher economic value than Project A. At the 10 percent level, Project B is economically feasible, and Project A is not. The results indicate that Project B is a better choice than Project A economically.

3. The Sensitivity Analysis in CBA

1. When the discount rate is 5 percent, the NPV is −$1,692, less than that at the 10 percent level, but still negative. Sometimes, it is informative to calculate the discount rate when the NPV is zero (the internal rate of return).
2. When the cost of ineffective replacement increases to $65, the NPV is positive and the purchase becomes economically feasible. In reality, the cost of ineffective replacement changes quite often, so a sensitivity analysis should be applied. In fact, when the discount rate is 10 percent, the NPV (when the cost of ineffective replacement = $20) = −$11,088; the NPV (when the cost of ineffective

replacement = $50) = –$3,614; the NPV (when the cost of ineffective replacement = $65) = $122; the NPV (when the cost of ineffective replacement = $100) = $8,838. So if the cost of ineffective replacement increases to $65, the NPV becomes positive.

3. An extended life increases the benefit. When the discount rate is 10 percent, the NPV (if the estimated project life = five years) = –$3,614; the NPV (if the estimated project life = six years) = –$1,600; the NPV (if the estimated project life = seven years) = $295. So, if the lifetime of the new system is extended to seven years, the NPV becomes positive.

4. Cost-Effectiveness Analysis

With a seven-year term and a 5 percent discount rate, the PVC per student for Option A is $22,689,230/1,600 = $14,181. The PVC per student for Option B is $22,227,076/1,500 = $14,818. Option A is more cost-effective (i.e., it is less expensive to educate each student).

Chapter 7. Financial Performance Monitoring

2. Obtaining Information from the CAFR

The following information was found in a city's CAFR:

1. Total assets for the primary entity: $1,563,967,486.
2. Total net assets for the primary entity: $928,959,123.
3. Total revenue for the primary entity (General Revenues + Program Revenues): $395,973,195.
4. Total expenses for the primary entity: $407,204,348.
5. Change in net assets for the primary entity: –$11,232,153.
6. Current assets for the primary entity (Total Assets – Noncurrent Assets): $576,876,178.
7. Total liabilities for the primary entity: $635,008,363.
8. Current liabilities for the primary entity (Total Liabilities – Noncurrent Liabilities): $149,320,759.

3. Calculation of Financial Indicators

1. Total revenue per resident: $395,973,195/194,913 = $2,032.
2. Total expenditure per resident: $407,204,348/194,913 = $2,089.

3. Current ratio: Current Assets/Current Liabilities = $576,876,178/ $149,320,759 = 3.86 (if the rule of thumb is 2, the liquidity of city appears to be in good shape by this measure).
4. Change in Net Assets/Total Net Assets = –$11,232,153/$928,959,123 = –0.012.
5. Total asset turnover: Total Revenue/Total Assets = $395,973,195/ $1,563,967,486 = 0.25.
6. Fixed asset turnover: Total Revenue/Fixed Assets = $395,973,195/ ($248,284,554 + $738,806,754) = $395,973,195/$987,091,308 = 0.40.
7. Return on assets: Change in Net Assets/Total Assets = –$11,232,153/ $1,563,967,486 = –0.007.

The city's negative change of net assets should cause concern. Financial monitoring of this indicator should be performed. The current ratio shows the city is in good standing in liquidity. The total asset turnover indicates that every dollar of the city's assets brings a quarter in revenue.

4. Historical Comparison of the Indicators

An examination of CAFRs for the past three years shows that the city had net asset increases two years in a row prior to this year's decline. The concern over the net asset decline of this year is alleviated a little. Nevertheless, the net asset change should be closely monitored. The analysis also shows that the change in the current ratio is in the territory of a normal change. The measure of the expenditure per resident indicates that city services have become more expensive for the past three years.

Chapter 8. Cash Management

2. Calculations

1. Using Excel, you should easily have: variance of net daily cash flows = $1,410.
2. Spread = $3 \times (0.75 \times 10 \times \$1,410/0.000274)^{1/3} = \$1,014$. Lower limit = $200. Upper limit = $1,214. Return point = $200 + ($1,014/3) = $538.

3. Cash Management in Bridgetown

1. To create a cash budget, you need to forecast monthly cash receipts and disbursements for the next year. A scan of the monthly cash flow data of the last three years does not show a clear trend for most

of the months. For example, the January receipt data of the past three years are $865,000, $873,650, and $871,903—the cash flow increases and then declines. Because there is no trend discovered in cash flows, you can use SMA in forecasting the cash receipts and disbursements for the next twelve months. You can then calculate net cash flows for every month by using forecast receipts minus disbursements: –$99,196 in January; $10,007 in February; $20,120 in March; $246,468 in April; $531,753 in May; –$187,115 in June; –$229,366 in July; $45,270 in August; –$30,180 in September; –$65,390 in October; $575,428 in November; and –$341,032 in December. The foundation also has a forecast average cash balance of $2,302,777.

2. The variance of monthly net cash flow with the above data is $79,744,304,424. Dividing it by thirty (the number of days in a month), we have the "variance of daily net cash flow": $2,658,143,481. From other information given, the spread $= 3 \times (0.75 \times 200 \times \$2,658,143,481/ 0.000137)^{1/3} = \$428,323$. Lower limit = $1,000,000. Upper limit = $1,428,323. Return point = $1,142,774

3. The foundation has a forecast average cash balance of $2,302,776. The Miller-Orr results indicate that the foundation can invest some of this money. One possible investment strategy suggested by the model is that the foundation always keep a minimum cash balance of $1,000,000, and, if the cash balance falls below it, replenish cash by an amount of $1,142,774 – $1,000,000 = $142,774. If the cash balance exceeds $1,428,323, the foundation should invest by the amount of $1,428,323 – $1,142,774 = $285,549.

Chapter 12. Financial Condition Analysis

2. Calculation

1. The correlation coefficients are: –0.196 between public safety expenditures and general government expenditures, 0.995 between public safety expenditures and total expenditures, and –0.248 between general government expenditures and total expenditures.

2. First, the data show that public safety expenditures are strongly positively associated with total expenditures. An increase in public safety expenditures leads to the increase in total expenditures. Second, there is a weak negative relationship between public safety expenditures and general government expenditures. In other words, the increase in public safety expenditures appears associated with

the decrease in general government expenditures. This result may suggest that general government activities compete resources with public safety activities.

3. Application

Analysis on Cash Solvency

Is there any warning trend in the cash ratio or the quick ratio? The values of the cash ratio for the past five years have been 3.42, 3.76, 4.25, 2.52, and 3.59. The values of the quick ratio have been 3.85, 4.30, 4.25, 2.52, and 3.63. Both indicators show that the city appears to have high liquidity. No clear trends are identified from this data, except that the ratios in Year 4 (2.52 for both the cash ratio and the quick ratio) appeared to be significantly lower than those of other years. Cash and cash-related assets were particularly low in that year, which deserves a close examination.

A correlation analysis has been conducted to specify the relationships between the cash ratio and assessed taxable values (the correlation coefficient = −0.33), population (−0.27), income per capita (−0.28), the unemployment rate (−0.43), and the millage (0.33), and between the quick ratio and assessed taxable values (−0.57), population (−0.54), income per capita (−0.48), unemployment rate (−0.57), and the millage (0.60). No strong relationship has been discovered. The cash solvency appears to be impacted by factors other than those included in this study. Further identification and examination of these factors are needed. The status of cash solvency in the city appears good now. However, the need for a good model to predict cash solvency will become more urgent when cash solvency deteriorates.

Budgetary Solvency

Budgetary solvency was discussed in the case study in this chapter.

Long-Run Solvency

The values of net asset ratio have increased for the past five years: 0.43, 0.46, 0.48, 0.51, and 0.54, which indicates that the city's long-run solvency by this measure has improved during that time. However, until information about other long-run solvency measures (such as the long-term debt ratio) becomes available for analysis, it is difficult to develop a complete picture of long-run solvency for the city.

The net asset ratio is strongly associated with assessed taxable values (the correlation coefficient = 0.99), population (0.99), and income per capita (0.98), which suggests that the increased values of these factors may improve the city's long-run solvency. Nevertheless, the positive relationship between the net asset ratio and the unemployment rate (0.86) is puzzling. Since only five years of data are analyzed, this relationship could be spurious. This finding needs to be reexamined when more data become available.

Service-Level Solvency

The values of net assets per capita have increased for the past five years: $3,337.90, $3,570.50, $3,770.20, $3,996.80, and $4,253.90. The city's service-level solvency by this measure has improved during this time. The net assets per capita appear to be associated with all of the socioeconomic/organizational factors in this study. But again, since only five years of data are used for analysis, these findings need to be reexamined when more data become available.

Index

XiaoHu Wang is associate professor of public administration at the University of Central Florida (UCF). He has degrees in public administration, economics, and business administration. Prior to his employment at UCF, he worked as a budget analyst for a number of governmental institutions. Wang's teaching and research focus on financial management and performance management in the public sector. His research has been published in the most prestigious academic journals in public administration and public finance.